BEATRIX FARRAND'S AMERICAN LANDSCAPES

Beatrix Jones Farrand (from the cover of the last issue of the *Reef Point Gardens Bulletin,* published after her death in 1959). Courtesy of Dumbarton Oaks, Trustees for Harvard University.

BEATRIX FARRAND'S AMERICAN LANDSCAPES

Her Gardens and Campuses

BY

DIANA BALMORI

DIANE KOSTIAL McGUIRE

ELEANOR M. McPECK

SAGAPRESS, INC.

SAGAPONACK, NEW YORK

Library of Congress Cataloging in Publication Data

Balmori, Diana.
Beatrix Farrand's American landscapes.

"A Ngaere Macray book"—
Bibliography: p.
Includes index.
1. Farrand, Beatrix, 1872–1959. 2. Landscape architecture—United States—History. 3. Landscape architects—United States—Biography. I. McGuire, Diane Kostial. II. McPeck, Eleanor M. III. Title.
SB470F.37B35 1985 712'.092'4 [B] 85-1969
ISBN 0-89831-003-2

Edited by Lois Fern
Designed by Joe Marc Freedman
Typeset by Graphic Composition, Inc., Athens, Georgia
Printed in Hong Kong
Third Printing 1993

Distributed by
Timber Press
9999 S.W. Wilshire
Portland, OR 97225
Orders and returns to above

CONTENTS

ACKNOWLEDGMENTS

LESLIE CLOSE, Director of the American Garden History Program at Wave Hill, deserves the credit for the collaboration that caused this book to be written. With the support of Peter Sauer, Executive Director of Wave Hill, she spent two years organizing a major exhibition of Beatrix Farrand's work. Among the professionals she brought together to help with the project were the authors of this book, each of whom has studied a different aspect of Farrand's work. Lois Fern, as the editor and indexer, has woven together the work of three authors and many photographers and has earned everyone's great respect. Marjorie Lightman, Executive Director of the Institute for Research in History, New York City, provides the Introduction, which illuminates the social and cultural context for Farrand's life and work. The information in the appendices is taken almost verbatim from an unpublished catalogue of the Beatrix Farrand Documents Collection at the University of California, Berkeley, that was compiled by Meredith Shedd.

Thanks are also due to the many people at Wave Hill who have helped: Antonia Adezio, Marco Polo Stufano, Eric Siegel, Lynn Leiner, Estelle Safran, Rosemary Palczewski, Annette Joseph, Earl Tucker, Suki Ports, Anthony Jennette, Robin Parkinson, and Margi Conrads.

Staff of the following institutions have generously contributed to both research and the implementation of the book and the exhibition: Dumbarton Oaks; the Documents Collection of the Department of Landscape Architecture, University of California, Berkeley; the Rockefeller Archive; the Pierpont Morgan Library; the New York Public Library; Yale University; Princeton University; the University of Chicago; the Santa Barbara Botanic Garden; Temple University; Cornell University; and the California Institute of Technology. Individuals who have been of particular assistance are named in the acknowledgments that precede each author's notes at the back of this volume.

This project was made possible by grants from the National Endowment for the Arts, the National Endowment for the Humanities, the New York Council on the Arts, and the J. M. Kaplan Fund.

NGAERE MACRAY
Sagapress, Inc.

WAVE HILL is a public garden overlooking the Hudson River in the Riverdale section of the Bronx. Its horticultural, educational, and visual and performing arts programs have been available to the public since 1975.

The Wave Hill American Garden History Program was begun in 1980. Its purpose is to promote interest in the study of American garden history by the general public and professionals. The program has grown, and through its conferences and exhibitions Wave Hill has become a locus for activities in American garden history.

PETER SAUER
Executive Director, Wave Hill

BEATRIX FARRAND'S AMERICAN LANDSCAPES

INTRODUCTION

MARJORIE LIGHTMAN

By dint of imagination and craft, historians have moved women of the late nineteenth and early twentieth centuries from the shadows of a forgotten past into the illuminated panorama of formal history. Pressed to recreate the lives of women and lacking the kinds of records accorded to kings, generals, and judges, historians have drawn on sources that describe large groups to create aggregate portraits of different kinds of women. The aggregate biographies have acquired further substance through the study of letters, diaries, and literature by and about women in different social classes, ethnic groups, and economic circumstances. Research over the past fifteen years has traced the rapid growth of a college-educated female population that redefined women's professional opportunities in the decades between 1880 and 1920. It has revealed how the largely immigrant-based industrial workforce posed critical social problems that became the focus of reformist activities, led often by women, and it has documented the gradual change in women's self-consciousness which came to include a demand for civil rights, culminating in the push for suffrage, finally won in the United States in 1920.

Beatrix Jones Farrand was born into neither the working class nor the middle class. She never went to college; she was not a crusading social reformer or an activist in the feminist cause. Yet the new scholarship is relevant for understanding the professional life of Beatrix Farrand as a landscape architect whose career spanned the "country-place era" of the early twentieth century, the Depression, and two world wars. Her childhood, her education, her choice of profession, and the manner in which she organized and ran her business can all be examined in the light of the insights and information provided by the new research. Such research provides background for the life of a woman who was very much her own person.

Beatrix Jones Farrand was born into that group among the wealthy for whom convention and manners allowed a wide latitude in personal life. Her parents were divorced at a time when divorce was anathema in the middle class and desertion was the poor man's escape from responsibility. After the divorce, Beatrix and her mother lived in a brownstone at a fashionable New York address on 11th Street. During these years her mother was a friend and correspondent of Henry James, and she also retained a close relationship with Edith Wharton, her former husband's sister. At home in artistic circles, Minnie Jones used her intelligence, charm, and social position to create a salon remembered in the history of literary New York, and along the way she earned an irregular income as a literary agent for her former sister-in-law.

The young Beatrix came of age at a time when women had only a limited number of options. Most traditional would have been to marry a man within her own social circle who would support her in a suitable fashion. She did not do so, for reasons we will probably never know. Certainly her parents' marriage had not provided a very happy model. Her mother, who was ill-prepared for life outside of marriage, may well have made clear through actions, if not words, that women needed to sustain themselves independently. Beatrix's Aunt Edith, a successful writer whose career was her passion and for whom marriage had also been an unhappy experience, provided yet another potent example of an independent adulthood. Moreover, the latter half of the nineteenth century was the first time when significant numbers of women entered the professions. Not coincidentally, this period also saw an increased opportunity for women to attend college, and among college-educated women more than fifty percent chose a single life, reinforcing, or perhaps creating, the belief that the pursuit of a career was antithetical to the roles of wife and mother.

A career, in the sense of earning a living through paid work, must be distinguished from meaningful work in the lives of American women of the late nineteenth century. Women's pursuit of activities within the realm of social reform, philanthropy, and the arts had a long, deeply embedded history in American culture and was not necessarily perceived as a conflict with the traditional roles of marriage and motherhood—as long as these activities were not all-consuming. Abolition, temperance, eugenics, education, consumer protection, as well as the traditional charities supported by churches and a rich array of cultural activities, all fit within the purview of a traditional woman's world. The last half of the century is rife with examples of women who worked in a sustained and directed manner over long periods of time and who achieved notable success in one or another of these fields.

Successfully earning a living was more difficult and certainly more fraught with role conflicts. For poor women, the burgeoning factories of the period provided paid work, however inadequate the pay and oppressive the working conditions. For these women, there was never any choice. Middle-class women found an outlet for their talents and educational skills in primary and secondary schools, rapidly increasing in number. Although teaching was always "respectable" work for middle- or upper-class women, it usually carried little better pay than the factory. By the last quarter of the century, the spread of the settlement-house movement began to offer middle- and upper-class women yet another avenue of work. While they were welcomed, and indeed were valuable contributors, to the development of social services, they were rarely paid, and when paid, the amount was generally insufficient to allow them to attain any real financial independence. Beatrix Farrand exhibited no particular interest in or inclination for the fields of teaching or social reform. But if not teaching or social service, why gardens?

The traditional dependence on the land for subsistence made gardens an integral part of nineteenth-century American life, even though large gardens where the purpose was primarily ornamental had been historically less a part of the American than the European tradition. During the late years of the century, however, when industrialism produced a new class of the wealthy, their estates came to include ornamental gardens as symbols of both wealth and of the European culture that was avidly sought with wealth. The decades before the Depression were a "golden moment for . . . landscape architecture." Stonework, statuary, fountains, and pools based on

French, Italian, and Spanish models became centerpieces for elaborate gardens covering the acres surrounding the new American country estates of the wealthy. Strong Anglophile traditions also characteristic of the American upper class resulted in a spread of the recent English fashion in rose and perennial gardens at the so-called "cottages" dotting the Atlantic shore from Maine to Southampton. Women played an important role in these developments, for gardens served as places to express beauty and to satisfy practical needs for herbs and vegetables, an extension of nurturing responsibilities as traditional as caring for the home. Farrand's aunt, Edith Wharton, an avid gardener, personified this upper-class, practical, and aesthetic association with gardens and gardening.

If gardening was at one and the same time a socially acceptable pursuit for a woman of Farrand's position and in accord with her personal inclinations, it was also a field at the edge of professionalization. Before the turn of the century, landscape gardening had appeared in the curriculum of several state universities. In 1900, Harvard began a program in landscape architecture and in 1916, the American Academy in Rome offered its first three-year fellowship in the field. The hitherto uncodified knowledge made part of the newly important university system was now available from credentialed professionals available for hire. In a pattern pervasive in the history of the professions, the development of programs within universities was accompanied by the organization of a professional association, in this case the American Society of Landscape Architects, founded in 1899.

Farrand was the only woman among the group that founded the society. Her education, however, had not come by way of the university. She followed a path which had more in common with the artist than with the scholar or scientist. Farrand left her girlhood home in New York for Boston where she studied with Charles Sprague Sargent at the arboretum he had created there. From him she learned about horticulture, as an artist would have apprenticed to a master to learn anatomy and the techniques of painting. She then traveled for several years in Europe studying gardens just as an aspiring artist would have studied paintings of past masters and schools. Like the artist, she kept notebooks of observations, impressions, and information, all of which contributed to her mastery of the art of gardens grafted upon her knowledge of plant life. From this education she evolved a unique style that nevertheless reflected the traditions her eye had become trained to see and value.

The analogy to the artist is all too fitting. Most artists were not women, nor were most landscape architects. Women, however, were to have a distinctive place in the historical evolution of professional landscape gardening. The Lowthrope School of Landscape Gardening for Women, founded in 1901 by Judith Motley Low, and the Cambridge School of Architecture and Landscape Architecture, founded in 1915 by Henry Atherton Frost and Bremer Pond, reflected the demand by women for the training which, at Harvard for example, had been reserved exclusively for men. Both schools educated an illustrious generation of women landscape architects for whom Low, Gertrude Jekyll, and Beatrix Jones Farrand were the role models. For this earlier generation, however, no amount of success erased the pervasive discrimination expressed toward women professionals. A *New York Times* article of 13 March 1938 noted that "people . . . who admire the scope of work done at Princeton and Yale will find it difficult to realize that these huge undertakings are directed by a woman, Mrs. Beatrix Cadwalader Jones Farrand." Nor was any formal training available to them in their youth. Farrand's years of travel in Europe were an independent learning experience made possible by her native intelligence, her determination, and her inherited means and social position.

European travel was a luxury, far different in every respect from what it was to become in the late twentieth century. It bespoke a life of leisure that allowed people to cross the ocean and spend months, even years, visiting and living abroad. Edith Wharton, for instance, spent the greater part of her adult life in Europe. In the last decades of the nineteenth century, a young woman of standing who traveled in Europe moved among an international set of family friends. Passed hand-to-hand and city-to-city, so to speak, she gained through her family name and connections entree to circles that both welcomed her and shared her presumed interest in culture. A stay of several years in Europe was a part of the standard education that had been given, for example, to the well-born Eleanor Roosevelt—whose uncle, Theodore Roosevelt, was, incidentally, a longtime friend of Farrand's aunt.

Farrand's adaptation of circumstances to pursue her own ends, which characterized her education, also characterized her business life. She began to practice her skill in landscape gardening by working with family friends, whose estates ranged up and down the east coast from Long Island to Newport to Maine. Her first office was in her mother's house in New York. For these early years it is not quite accurate to call her work a business; it was more a cottage industry. Like poor women who took in piecework, minded children, or took in boarders, she charged fees for her services, but her costs were to some degree hidden since she supported neither an independent establishment nor a regular staff.

To move from this type of undertaking to an independent business, Farrand needed both a base of clients large enough to provide a steady cashflow and the capital to buy furnishings and provide a financial cushion for periods when work was slow. Her growing reputation for fine work among family friends gained her a network of referrals which quickly assumed a professional, rather than familial, character. Certainly her business appeared a promising gamble, and her aunt appears to have provided the capital essential for expansion. When Farrand opened her own offices, she moved beyond social norms for women of her background by transforming an interest and skill that had been the pursuit of a young woman whose work, even when compensated, had the appearance of friendship, into a more fully cash-nexus relationship with clients who were not necessarily of her circle. She moved from the security of the middle- and upper-class social ethic that encouraged women to undertake meaningful and useful work, especially if unmarried, into the world of career women.

By the early years of the twentieth century, the pattern of Farrand's business life was set. In many ways her manner of work was a model for later developments in the organization of similar consulting firms, which by their nature revolve around the reputation, skill, and appeal of their principal. Her main office was in New York. Her clientele was spread across the nation and even reached to England—a business as cosmopolitan as her upbringing and education. As estate work dwindled, beginning after World War I and into the Depression years, she undertook more college and university work. Perhaps her greatest garden was Dumbarton Oaks, begun in 1921 and spanning the remaining twenty-five years of her professional life. She appears always to have firmly controlled the projects she undertook. She worked directly with clients while her staff—an extension of her arms, legs, and eyes—worked to realize her ideas. Farrand always remained her own chief salesperson and it was for her that the client paid. However, her ability to delegate work and to divide activities so that staff could be responsible for subsections of a project multiplied the pieces of work she could undertake. Her careful records of working time, materials, and expenses, provided the information she needed in order to bill enough to cover her indirect costs and costs of maintaining an office. The skillful marketing of her name and services over the years created a cachet in having a Farrand garden that allowed her to charge what was undoubtedly top price for her services.

These very same factors raise speculation about how her business fit with the traditions of women in American society. For example, she never took a full partner into her firm. In a consulting business, be it architectural, legal, financial, or landscape gardening, partners can increase the income potential exponentially. Thus a firm of three partners does not simply produce three times the income or increase the working capacity threefold. It reduces the costs to each partner since the necessary support services for one professional, especially in an office organized to divide tasks among a group or staff, does not double for two or triple for three. Quite the contrary, the cost per project decreases. On the other hand, the control of any one partner is proportionally less than in an independent practice. Farrand's control would have diminished in a partnership.

Certainly there are men as well as women who exercise control and who seek independent practices. Nonetheless, for a woman there is an added component. Should her partners be men, the woman would be in a disadvantaged position, regardless of her professional stature, simply by virtue of the pervasive character of women's secondary roles. On the other hand, if the firm had several female partners, its perceived status as a women's firm would have even further complicated the acceptance of Farrand as an expert who happened to be a woman.

There was yet another and perhaps more critical factor, which went to the core of Farrand's business organization. It has always been a general business axiom to realize a maximum return. It is unclear that this was Farrand's goal. Certainly she sought good compensation for her work; but she also carefully chose her work. Her attention to the quality of the plantings and the long-term personal supervision of her gardens ran against maximizing her income. A partner might have insisted on compromising her standards.

In the end, the measure of a successful business is its survival. By this measure Farrand was among the most successful of her contemporaries. While many landscape-architecture firms failed after the crash in 1929, Farrand succeeded in shifting much of her work from private estates to institutions. The lack of a partner, however, assured that her business would not outlive her own professional life, even though it had successfully outlived depression and war. In this way her professional life paralleled those of social reformers like Grace Dodge, who withdrew from Columbia Teacher's College when it became a professional pedagogical institution, or Josephine Shaw Lowell, who sought intellectual rigor in philanthropy, but who, like Farrand, failed to create an institution in her own name. Perhaps Farrand never meant to create a business that would outlive her; rather, her business was a means to shape her passion into work that was a compromise between her circumstances, her times, and her talents. She was a professional whose legacy is the careful documentation of her work and the living gardens she created.

Beatrix Farrand with landscape gardener William Robinson at his home, Gravetye Manor, in England. Courtesy of University of California, Berkeley; Department of Landscape Architecture; Documents Collection.

1. Mary Cadwalader Rawle, about 1865, from the portrait by William Oliver Stone.

A BIOGRAPHICAL NOTE AND A CONSIDERATION OF FOUR MAJOR PRIVATE GARDENS

ELEANOR M. McPECK

BIOGRAPHICAL NOTE[1]

Beatrix Jones Farrand, the finest woman landscape architect of her generation, was born in New York City on 19 June 1872, the only child of Mary Cadwalader Rawle and Frederic Rhinelander Jones. Her father, the son of George Frederic Jones and Lucretia Rhinelander, was Edith Wharton's oldest brother. Wharton's biographer, R. W. B. Lewis, says that Frederic and Edith "had nothing in common."[2] A shadowy figure, about whom almost nothing is known, Jones became, after his divorce from Mary Cadwalader, a longtime resident of Paris, where he died at the age of seventy-two. Mary Cadwalader came from an old-line Philadelphia family. Her ancestors had lived in or near Philadelphia for over a hundred years. She spoke French well, had traveled abroad, and was an omnivorous reader, "always animated" in conversation and "often brilliant," according to friends.[3] She appeared to a young visitor to have had "quick sympathetic eyes." An early portrait (fig. 1) reveals a lovely looking young woman. "Freddy" and Mary were married in Philadelphia in 1870 and came to live in New York City in a comfortable brownstone on East 11th Street. The marriage was not a success and ended in divorce before Beatrix was twelve.

Early Life

Growing up in the highly structured world of New York society, Beatrix's early life cannot have been entirely happy, given the circumstances, nor was it dull. Tutored at home, as many young women of her social class were, she frequently traveled abroad with her mother and with her aunt, Edith Wharton. She often accompanied her uncle, John Lambert Cadwalader, an ardent lover of sport, on shooting trips in Scotland. Cadwalader (fig. 2), a distinguished New York lawyer and a trustee of the Metropolitan Museum of Art and the New York Zoological Society, was instrumental in founding the New York Public Library. He had served also as a member of the Board of Trustees of the Astor Library prior to its consolidation with the Lennox and Tilden libraries to form the New York Public Library, and he continued as a trustee of the consolidated library from its formation until his death in 1914, serving for a time as its president. He took particular interest in founding the Print Department and left to the library his personal collection of British mezzotints and engravings—pictures of rural life and sporting scenes.

Cadwalader was known for "his singular force of character, his energy and intelligence, his wide knowledge of the world, his independence of thought, his wit and cordiality."[4] He undoubtedly acted as Beatrix's surrogate father and is said to have recognized in his niece an early talent for landscape and "an indomitable will." "Let her be a gardener or, for that matter, anything she wants to be. What she wishes to do will be well done."[5]

Beatrix's childhood world has been well characterized by Henry James's biographer, Leon Edel, as a "tight little world with . . . old decencies, . . . stratified codes, [and a] tradition of elegance."[6] This was, as Edith Wharton later put it, "a life of leisure and aimiable hospitality."[7] Her mother seems to have kept one of the liveliest salons in New York. "Minnie," as she was called by close friends, acted in response to reduced financial circumstances as part-time literary agent for her sister-in-law, Edith, and kept within her immediate circle some of the best literary and artistic minds of the period, including Brooks and Henry Adams, Marion Crawford, and John La Farge. She was asked by Brooks Adams to revise his introduction to Henry Adams's *Degradation of the Democratic Dogma* and was for a long time Henry James's close correspondent. It was to Minnie Jones that James delivered his

2. John Lambert Cadwalader; drawing by John Singer Sargent. Courtesy of New York Public Library, Prints Division.

famous statement that Edith Wharton "must be tethered in native pastures, even if it reduce her to a backyard in New York."[8] James often stayed with Minnie when he came to New York, enjoying the "safety and comfort"[9] of her house on East 11th Street. In a letter to Minnie, dated 1905, he referred to her as his "benefactress" and sent his love to Beatrix, "the Earth-shaker."[10]

Minnie's friend, Mrs. Winthrop Chanler, offered further impressions of the atmosphere at East 11th Street in her book *Roman Spring.* "Her house . . . was full of books and old engravings. . . . On the second story were two pleasant rooms that she called her 'Authors' Suite,' where she made her friends very comfortable. . . . [The house] combined all creature comforts with a sense of civilized tradition and intellectual resource."[11] It was within this obviously protected, often animated environment that Beatrix spent her formative years. She must have felt isolated as the only child of divorced

3. Beatrix Jones [Farrand] in 1896, portrait by S.C. Sears. Courtesy of University of California, Berkeley; Department of Landscape Architecture.

parents, but her mother—whom she later described as "the best companion, wise, kindly, brave, witty and distinguished"[12]—provided the affection and sense of security she needed.

The Education of a Landscape Gardener

What persuaded Beatrix Jones (fig. 3) to become a landscape architect? Throughout her long career, as her close associate, architect and landscape architect Robert Patterson, has written, she preferred to call herself a "landscape gardener" rather than a "landscape architect."[13] By her own account, she was "the product of five generations of garden lovers."[14] Her grandmother had owned one of the first espaliered fruit gardens in Newport. And at the age of eight, Beatrix had observed the laying-out of the grounds at her parents' summer place, Reef Point, at Bar Harbor, Maine. Reef Point, which she later inherited, became one of the most ambitious gardening projects of her career.

There are indications that Beatrix at one time studied music. She may have studied drawing in Berlin when she was abroad. Two watercolor studies dated 1892, "Wall, Jardin de Tuileries" and "Wall, Rue de L'Abbaye," possibly in her own hand, indicate that at about the age of twenty she may have studied at the Académie des Beaux Arts in Paris. The decisive moment in respect to her ultimate profession occurred in 1892, when, by her account, "a fortunate meeting with Mrs. Charles Sargent [a friend of her mother's] changed the course of a young woman's life."[15] Mary Sargent's husband, Charles Sprague Sargent, then the dean of American horticulture, was the founder and first director of the Arnold Arboretum near Boston. It was Charles Sargent who suggested that Beatrix study landscape gardening, and she came soon after this meeting to live at the Sargents' estate, Holm Lea, in Brookline (fig. 4). From Sargent she learned the basic principles of landscape design. She studied botany at the arboretum, learned how to survey and to stake out a piece of ground. Sargent advised her, wisely, "to make the plan fit the ground and not to twist the ground to fit a plan."[16]

Beatrix's journal of this period reveals her as a conscientious and observant student. On a visit to Frederick Law Olmsted's Brookline office, she noticed the "charming dell," but on the lawn were "two azalea, of fearful color, one blueish pink and the other bright orange."[17] Of the Boston Public Garden, she remarked: "The planting is very bad. There are many fine trees in the Garden but they do not show up for much as they are not led up to in any way nor is the multitude of small beds calculated to give repose to the eye & give breadth of effect."[18]

Following Sargent's advice to travel widely, Beatrix went abroad in 1895, spending the spring on the continent. Sailing first to Gibraltar, she proceeded with kodak in hand to Italy, making her base first in Rome and later in Florence. At the Villa Aldobrandini, she found the view of the campagna beautiful, admiring also "two twisted columns above the terrace"[19] and the remains of Fontana's great system of waterworks. On the afternoon of March 27th, after "a painful society morning in the American Colony" in Rome, she visited the gardens of the Colonna Palace.

4. Holm Lea, estate of Charles Sprague Sargent, about 1900.

> *Going up many flights of dark stairs, we came out on the old parterre. How much of it is the original design and how much reconstruction is hard to tell. From a central round fountain basin radiate eight or ten paths & instead of all the points coming together at the fountain, they are cut off by a circle of larger diameter than the rim of the fountain. Of course this leaves quite a good open space around the fountain, which gently trickles for the benefit of the people who may wish to sit on curved seats which follow the circle. The parterre is divided from what is now a little English garden, by a sunken alley bordered with box & laurel.*[20]

At the Villa Lante, she admired "the beautiful bronze fountain at the center of the parterre," noting that "in the little squares around the fountain were bowls with oleanders surrounded on three sides by high box hedges."[21] At Florence, the Boboli Gardens (fig. 5) left an enduring impression:

> *At the foot of the hill is the oval basin for the fountains. . . . These are admirably set in the oval of clipped ilex hedges which throw out their colors to the best advantage. It is in a place like this that the charm of the Italian garden is felt, with beautiful statues, charming in their graces, the dark & rich colors of the Italian trees, and the vista up the hill between old cypresses. . . . The whole garden is one of the most charming I have seen & one of the most refined.*[22]

In June of the same year, she went to England. She visited Kew three times, went to Hampton Court, Hyde Park, and Kensington Gardens, and on June 27th to Vita Sackville West's garden at Knole. Of significance in terms of her later work, were Beatrix's visits to Gertrude Jekyll and to Pens-

5. View in the Boboli Gardens, Florence. Courtesy of Graduate School of Design Library, Harvard University.

hurst, a garden much praised some years later by Jekyll in her book *Some English Gardens* (1904). Jekyll was then the leading exponent of cottage gardening. She was an advocate of the use of wild and native materials and was best known for her subtle and impressionistic use of color, an approach that had a substantial effect on Beatrix's work. "I am strongly for treating garden and wooded ground in a pictorial way," Jekyll wrote, "mainly with large effects, and in the second place with lesser beautiful incidents and for arranging plants and trees and grassy spaces so that they look happy and at home, and make no parade of conscious effort. I try for beauty and harmony everywhere, and especially for harmony of color."[23]

The ancient Tudor garden at Penshurst had been "confirmed and renewed," in Jekyll's phrase, at the end of the nineteenth century (fig. 6). Beatrix found there several features later incorporated in her own garden designs. The handsome gate piers, wrought-iron urns, and clipped yews suggested a diffused version of the classical gardens she had recently seen in Italy. The terrace at Penshurst was formal in aspect, though softened by lawn and picturesquely placed trees and perennial borders. Here the English formal garden had been diffused by horticultural impressionism, a mode of gardening which would soon find its way to America.

During this formative period, Beatrix also began to collect early prints of gardens and books on architecture, botany, and landscape gardening. Her extensive library, which she kept in later years at Reef Point and finally donated to the University of California at Berkeley, included many rare illustrated volumes, among them Israel Silvestre's *Diverse Views of France, Rome and Florence* (1600) and Humphry Repton's *Observations on the Theory and Practice of Landscape Gardening* (1805). She also purchased William Robinson's *The Wild Garden* (1881), as well as copies of nearly all of Gertrude Jekyll's books, including *Wood and Garden* (1899).

During these years of observation and travel, Beatrix occasionally contributed reviews to Charles Sprague Sargent's *Garden and Forest.* A short notice entitled "Bridge over the Kent at Levens Hall" appeared in 1896.

> *The simple lines and quiet color of this ivy draped bridge in Westmoreland are what make it satisfying to the eye and an added charm to the stream; it is made with stone of the country and the native plants grow about it as*

6. The Terrace at Penshurst, Kent; watercolor by George S. Elgood (reproduced in Gertrude Jekyll, *Some English Gardens,* London, 1910).

> *familiarly as though it were a bowlder* [sic] *playfully deposited there by nature in the ice age.*

She noted too that bridges of this sort would be, of course, more durable than wooden constructions. The initial cost, to be sure, would be greater, but in the long run the stone would prove more economical.[24] Here was the constructive, observant mind at work, with an eye for picturesque effects and a preference for natural materials.

Early Practice

Beatrix Jones returned from her European travels in September of 1895 and soon afterward opened her first office, on the top floor of her mother's house on East 11th Street. She had been encouraged by Sargent to accept commissions, and she received what was probably her first important commission from William Garrison of Tuxedo, New York in 1896. Commissions from Trenor L. Park of Harrison, New York and Elizabeth Hope Slater of Newport followed in 1897 and 1898, respectively, and Beatrix Jones was soon considered one of America's outstanding landscape architects. On 4 January 1899—only three years after establishing her practice—she met in New York with Samuel Parsons, Jr., John C. Olmsted, Jr., and several others to found the American Society of Landscape Architects, organized in response to a need expressed by Warren Manning, Samuel Parsons, and Charles Eliot for a general association of landscape professionals in the United States. She was the only woman among the founders.

Interviewed shortly afterward by the *New York Herald Tribune,* she remarked:

> *Society yes, it is very agreeable . . . a little of it. I should be lost without sometimes sharing the diversions of my old friends. But to live for it and in it entirely. Oh, never. This is so different. It is work—hard work and at the same time it is perpetual pleasure. With this grand art of mine I do not envy the greatest painter, or sculptor or poet that lived. It seems to me that all arts are combined in this.*[25]

In her approach to landscape design, Beatrix seems to have taken a position somewhere between the formalists on the one hand and the naturalists on the other. The leading advocate of formalism in this country was Charles Platt, who had studied abroad and published an influential book entitled *Italian Villas and their Gardens* (1894). Platt placed chief emphasis upon the integral relationship between the house and the garden, advocating that the two should be designed and seen as a whole (fig. 7).

In the revival of classical taste, Edith Wharton and Ogden Codman were not far behind. In their book, *The Decoration of Houses* (1897), they asserted that "the best models were to be found in buildings erected in Italy after the beginning of the sixteenth century and in other European countries after the assimilation of the Italian influence."[26] They went on to say that "moderation, fitness, and relevance" were the qualities that gave perma-

7. The C.H. Sprague Garden, designed by Charles Platt about 1896. Courtesy of Graduate School of Design Library, Harvard University.

nence to works of architecture.[27] Edith Wharton gave more specific reference to these general principles in her later book *Italian Villas and Their Gardens* (1905):

> *The inherent beauty of the [Italian] garden lies in the grouping of its parts—in the converging of the lines of its long ilex-walks, the alternation of sunny open spaces with cool woodland shade, the proportion between terrace and bowling green, or between the height of a wall and the width of the path. . . . The great pleasure grounds overlooking the Roman Campagna are laid out on severe majestic lines: the parts are few; the total effect is one of breadth and simplicity.*[28]

Beatrix Jones seems to have been guided by these principles, and, in an article entitled "The Garden in Relation to the House," she expressed the view that "the arts of architecture and landscape gardening are sisters . . . not antagonists. . . . The work of the architect and landscape gardener should be done together from the beginning . . . not, as too often happens, one crowding the other out."[29] In a later article, she wrote:

> *The garden large or small must be treated in the impressionist manner. . . . The planting must be done on a big scale. The artist must try to keep step with the great stride of Nature and copy as far as may be her breadth and simplicity.*[30]

Beatrix's earliest designs were formal in character but they also reflected the influence of William Robinson, who, like Jekyll, advocated the use of wild and native materials. She shared with Jekyll a subtle and impressionistic use of color. Her associate Robert Patterson later wrote that her work "had a freedom of scale, a subtle softness of line and an unobtrusive asymmetry."[31]

Beatrix Jones Farrand gained among her clients a reputation for thoroughness and certainty of approach. At Dartington Hall, an English country estate of more than two thousand acres, she is said to have understood the complexities of the whole site and to have laid out within days of her first site visit, terraces, the great lawn and the encircling system of paths. This reputation extended to her public work at Princeton, Yale, and Chicago universities, where she sought to achieve broad, simple landscape effects that would withstand constant use by generations of college students.

Beatrix Jones married Max Farrand, a distinguished constitutional historian and chairman of the Yale History Department, on 17 December 1913. Thereafter she spent part of her time in New Haven, and part at her office in New York and her summer residence, Reef Point, in Bar Harbor. In 1927, Max Farrand was appointed Director of the Huntington Library in San Marino, California. He was elected president of the American Historical Association in 1940. He received honorary degrees from seven colleges and universities, including Princeton, Michigan and California. Described as "an imposing, broad shouldered figure," he was an enthusiastic golfer and freshwater fisherman.[32] Beatrix and Max Farrand were both dedicated to their work and their marriage seems to have been a happy and constructive partnership. Together they entertained members of the staff and visiting scholars in the Director's House on the Huntington Library grounds until Max's retirement in 1941.

Keeping in effect three offices simultaneously after her marriage to Max Farrand, one in New Haven (and later San Marino), another at Reef Point, and a third in New York City, Beatrix traveled constantly between offices and to visit clients in Maine, New York, Washington, D.C., and elsewhere, supervising the planting and construction of her garden designs. Her three principal assistants, Anne Baker, Margaret Bailie, and, after 1929, Ruth Havey worked with the rest of the staff in New York. Maintaining what must have been an exhausting schedule, Beatrix worked long hours on the train and in hotel rooms. Robert Patterson and others have said that she rarely drew.

> *She preferred to prepare a planting plan alone in her sitting room, a landscape clear on her inner eye, arranging her palette by writing plant names on a half bushel of white labels. Sorted into bundles, the labels were taken to the job and parceled out to gardeners and assistants.*[33]

Michael Straight, the son of an early client who later employed her himself, remembers her well in his own garden in Alexandria, Virginia, "striding about and giving orders to the head gardener, a magnificent Scotsman, very austere, in her long skirt and high lace collar."[34]

Farrand brought to her art a discriminating and critical intelligence that earned her the respect of her contemporaries. She received many honors, including awards from the Garden Club of America (1947) and the New York Botanical Garden. Formal and reserved in both appearance and manner, she was admired for her integrity, dedication, and her exceptional talent as a landscape architect.

Beatrix devoted the last years of her life to Reef Point Gardens, a project that she and her husband developed on the family property she had inherited from her mother at Bar Harbor, Maine. Hoping to leave behind her an institution designed for both scholarly and experimental purposes, she continued this work after her husband's death in 1945. Reef Point ultimately included a test garden of native flora, a rare collection of single roses (thought to be the most complete in this country), and a working library (which included, among other materials, original garden plans of Gertrude Jekyll and an herbarium). In 1955, Farrand decided that the future of Reef

8. Sketch for Lych Gate, 1897. Courtesy of University of California, Berkeley; Department of Landscape Architecture; Documents Collection.

Point was not secure. Acting with her usual energy and dispatch, she sold the house and gardens, moving many of the plants to a nearby garden. She donated the contents of her library, her office correspondence, and her garden plans to the Department of Landscape Architecture at the University of California at Berkeley, where they are preserved today. She remained at Bar Harbor until her death on 27 February 1959.

PRIVATE GARDENS

The Formative Years (1896–1913)

Of Beatrix Jones Farrand's earliest work we have only secondary evidence, since all of her private gardens from the period between 1896 and 1913 have been lost or destroyed. It is possible to form some idea of the direction and quality of her work through surviving plans, sketches and drawings.

9. Preliminary study for the grounds of William R. Garrison, Tuxedo, New York, 1896. Courtesy of University of California, Berkeley; Department of Landscape Architecture; Documents Collection.

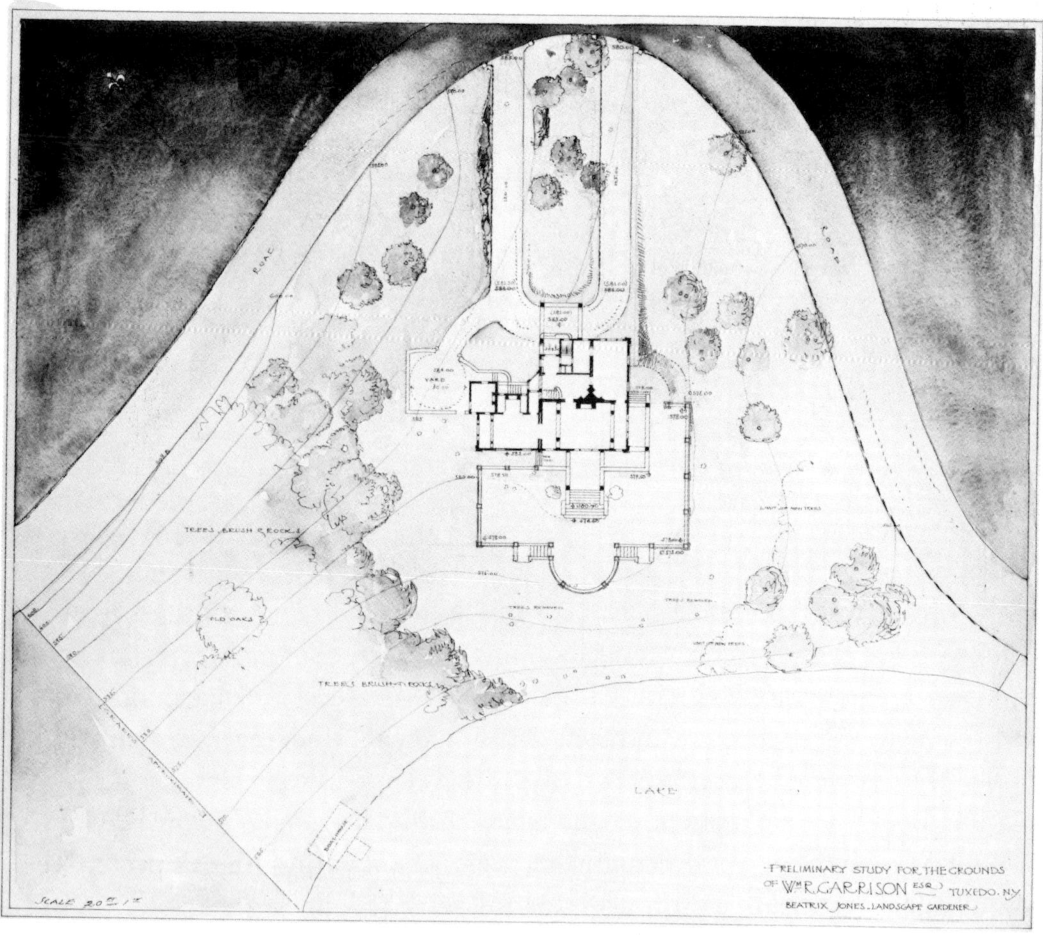

10. Sketch for the grounds of William R. Garrison, 1896. Courtesy of University of California, Berkeley; Department of Landscape Architecture; Documents Collection.

A watercolor sketch (fig. 8), possibly in her own hand, for the so-called Lych Gate at Seal Harbor, Maine, commissioned in 1897, indicates an early preference for rustic, well-crafted architectural detail. This charming drawing seems to relate directly, in terms of its character and spirit, to her article published the year before, "Bridge over the Kent at Levens Hall."

A preliminary plan (fig. 9) and a sketch (fig. 10) for William R. Garrison, of Tuxedo, New York, dated 1896, indicate the young Jones's preference for classical structure within an informal setting. The high, gabled house rests on an imposing and massive stone terrace which projects boldly and

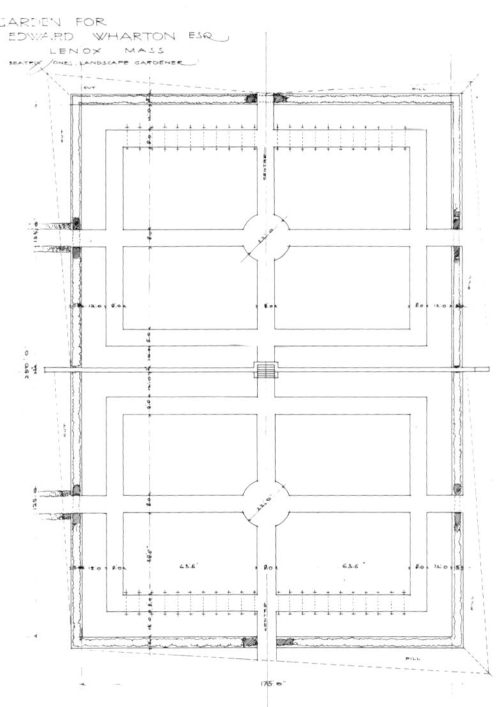

11. Schematic plan for Edward Wharton, Lenox, Massachusetts, 1901. Courtesy of University of California, Berkeley; Department of Landscape Architecture; Documents Collection.

12. Schematic plan for Edward Whitney, Oyster Bay, Long Island, New York, 1912. Courtesy of University of California, Berkeley; Department of Landscape Architecture; Documents Collection.

1. SHRUB PLANTING
2. IRIS . TALL GROWING VARIETIES NEAR SHRUBS -
3. GRASS. WALKS -
4. EXISTING TREES -

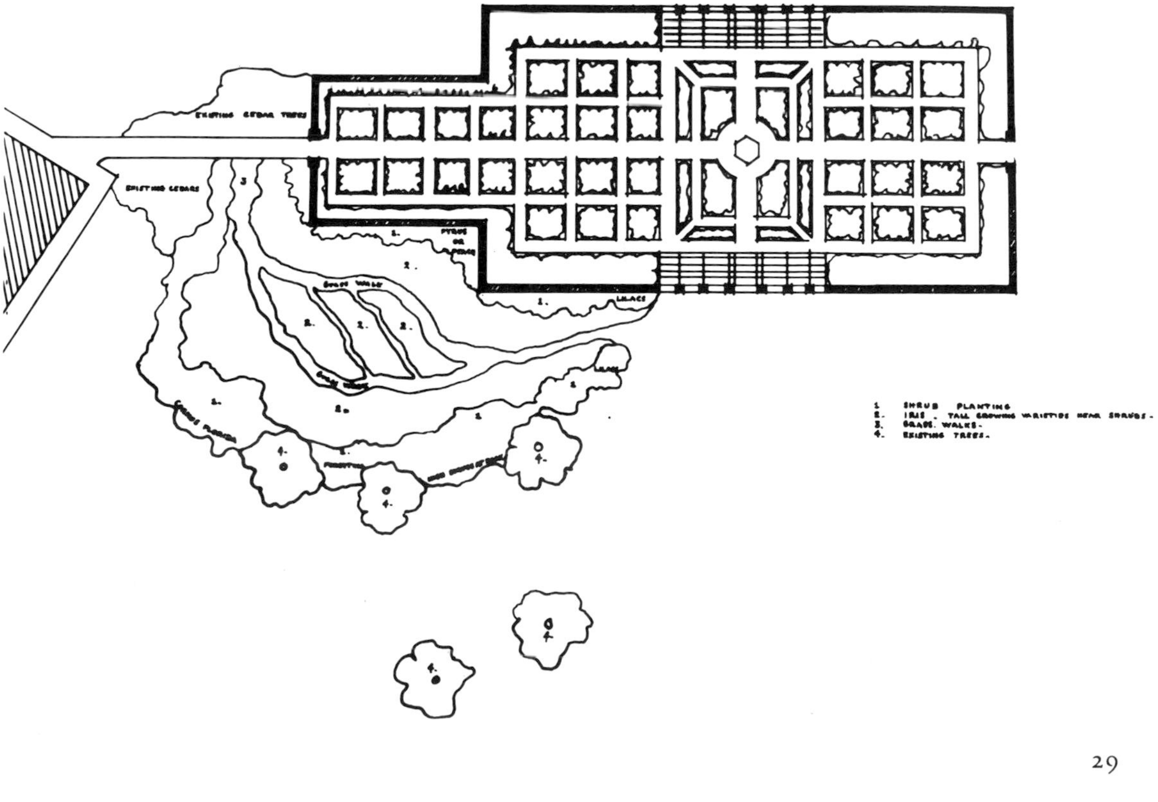

13. Plan for a suburban garden, 1910. Courtesy of University of California, Berkeley; Department of Landscape Architecture; Documents Collection.

14. Perspective for a suburban garden, 1910. Courtesy of University of California, Berkeley; Department of Landscape Architecture; Documents Collection.

with authority onto the landscape, overlooking the lake and neoclassic boathouse below.

Also belonging to the formative years are a plan (pl. I) and watercolor sketches for Clement Newbold of Jenkintown, Pennsylvania, dating from around 1901. Here we see geometrically composed parterres enclosed by a low, stone wall. Several Italianate elements, the pergola and arbors, have been reinterpreted through the use of local stone and native wood. Well-placed sculpture, fountains, and pools were to become part of her standard design vocabulary.

The schematic plan for Edward Wharton dated 14 July 1901 (fig. 11) indicates again Jones's tendency to organize her designs along well-defined classical lines. As in a later plan for Harris Fahnestock of Lenox, Massachusetts (1910), we see parterres enclosed by a stone wall. A more complex version is the schematic plan for Edward F. Whitney dating from shortly after 1906 (fig. 12). Here, as in so many of her subsequent plans, we see an attempt to reconcile both formal and informal elements. An informal wood and iris garden are juxtaposed against the strictly organized parterre with flanking arbors.

In a hypothetical scheme produced in 1910 for an Architectural League competition for "An Ideal Suburban Place," Beatrix attempted to extend this same, basic design vocabulary to a small suburban lot. Of this scheme, she wrote:

> *No attempt has been made at an informal or so called naturalistic treatment because on a lot less than half an acre in size and with a house of the type shown here, irregular lines, winding walks and scattered trees would only look crowded without giving any illusion of space. Honesty and clearness of design are perhaps even more necessary in the treatment of the small places than they are in larger areas, where the size of the grounds alone gives a suggestion of distancy which is impossible to ever obtain in a little lot. Here a frank recognition of the boundary line is essential.*[35]

In her plan (figs. 13 & 14), "fence and hedge give seclusion to the back yard which is simply a lawn, with croquet possibilties, bordered with flowers and a gravel walk with shade trees at each corner."[36] Here the grand scale usually associated with Beatrix Farrand's work (fig. 15) has been reduced for middle-income consumption. The trademarks, however, are there—clarity of outline, a strong sense of enclosure, the simple plan enriched by architectural detail and softened by perennial beds and trees, that give "spots of shade on sultry days." Finally she writes, with characteristic concern for economy:

> *It has been taken for granted in making plans and suggestions for planting that the house is to be a home for all the year round and not merely a place visited two or three months of the summer and the object has been to keep the original cost and subsequent outlay for the maintenance of the grounds as low as consistent with a comfortable and permanent home.*[37]

15. View of the house and garden of Harris Fahnestock, about 1910. Courtesy of Sheila Scott.

Beatrix Jones had firmly established her practice by 1913. Given the social context of her world and the particular requirements of her clients, whose background corresponded with her own, she was ideally suited to design gardens for that amiable and hospitable society which nearly vanished after World War II. Her clients were equally at home in town, abroad, or in their country places on the coasts of Maine or Long Island. Two garden designs, one for a town house, the other for a country estate, both done after 1914, offer further understanding of her professional approach and working methods.

The Pierpont Morgan Town House, New York City; Now the Pierpont Morgan Library (1913–1943)

Beginning in 1913, shortly before her marriage to Max Farrand, Beatrix Jones was commissioned to supervise the grounds surrounding J. Pierpont Morgan's town house at 36th Street and Madison Avenue in New York City. The commission probably came through the influence of her uncle, John Cadwalader, who was a frequent shooting companion of Morgan's. Morgan died within months of Beatrix's assignment, but she remained in charge of the gardens at the request of his son, the younger J. P. Morgan. Working from her Bar Harbor office and from her New York office at 124 East 40th Street near the Morgan property, she designed the original town-house garden and supervised all construction, planting, and maintenance. She was also responsible for a subsequent garden, modified in 1924, associated with the Morgan Library and now owned by the Lutheran Church in America. A review of her office correspondence with the Morgan family over the period from 1914 to 1943[38] provides a revealing glimpse of Farrand's method of work, the thoroughness with which she approached every aspect of design and maintenance.

Writing to Beatrix Farrand shortly after his father's death in December 1914, Morgan, Jr. remarked:

> *The garden certainly look[ed] nicely this autumn and I was very interested to see Condon [the gardener] the other morning planting at a great rate in the beds. It did occur to me however that he planted . . . rather hastily into holes made by a long pointed stick. I have always understood that his was not the ideal arrangment for bulbs, whose roots I understand, should be in soft earth, and not into pockets in hard earth. However, perhaps I do Condon an injustice. I did not get out there and see what he was at.*
>
> *I hope you will go on and do as you have done heretofore with the garden; also that you will come in some afternoon and have tea with Mrs. Morgan and me, on your way to the train or at any time that you have an opportunity.*

Farrand replied the following week:

I am glad to be told about Condon's method of planting bulbs, although I think if he followed my directions as to spading the beds, that there would not be much trouble in the actual result of the bulbs next spring. Condon certainly has kept the garden looking a little more tidy this autumn and he is getting constantly poked up. . . . I am glad you want me to keep on with the garden and I think you will find that there has been a very material reduction in the expense of running it this year.

Economy appears in Farrand's correspondence with the younger Morgan from the beginning, and throughout their twenty-year association it was a consistent and troublesome theme. Scrupulous in every detail, Farrand submitted semiannual accounts outlining every dollar spent. A summary of her bill for the period from July 1 to December 31, 1920 is typical:

October 3–9, to Gaston Petit, for wages, $30.00
October 8, to C. H. Tetty Co., for packing and delivery of 930 Chrysanthemums, $487.00
October 12, to Jos. Cahill for Removing Rubbish, $5.00
Henry Mulvaney for six loads of manure, $90.00
November 26, to Cottage Gardens Co. for 27 evergreens, $157.00
December 17, to Gaston Petit, petty cash for buying salt hay for the flower beds, $25.00, etc.

Farrand's annual bill for supervision of this work was $1000.00.

Of the design of the original town-house garden, which extended between the two Morgan houses on Madison Avenue between 36th and 37th streets, only faint photographic record survives. It is possible to reconstruct an idea of the planting, however, from several sketches and from bills paid (to Cottage Gardens Co. Inc., for example, on 15 April 1920, for 15 *Rhododendron maximum,* 15 *Rhododendron cawtabiense album,* 5 *Rhododendron album elegans,* 40 *Juniperus pfiteriana,* 15 *Pinus mugho,* 5 *Andromeda japonica,* 20 *Ilex crenata,* and 12 *Forsythia).*

Beginning in 1924, with the opening of the Morgan Library, the once private garden became public. And it was subsequent to this time that Farrand produced a series of plans which give a clearer picture of what the

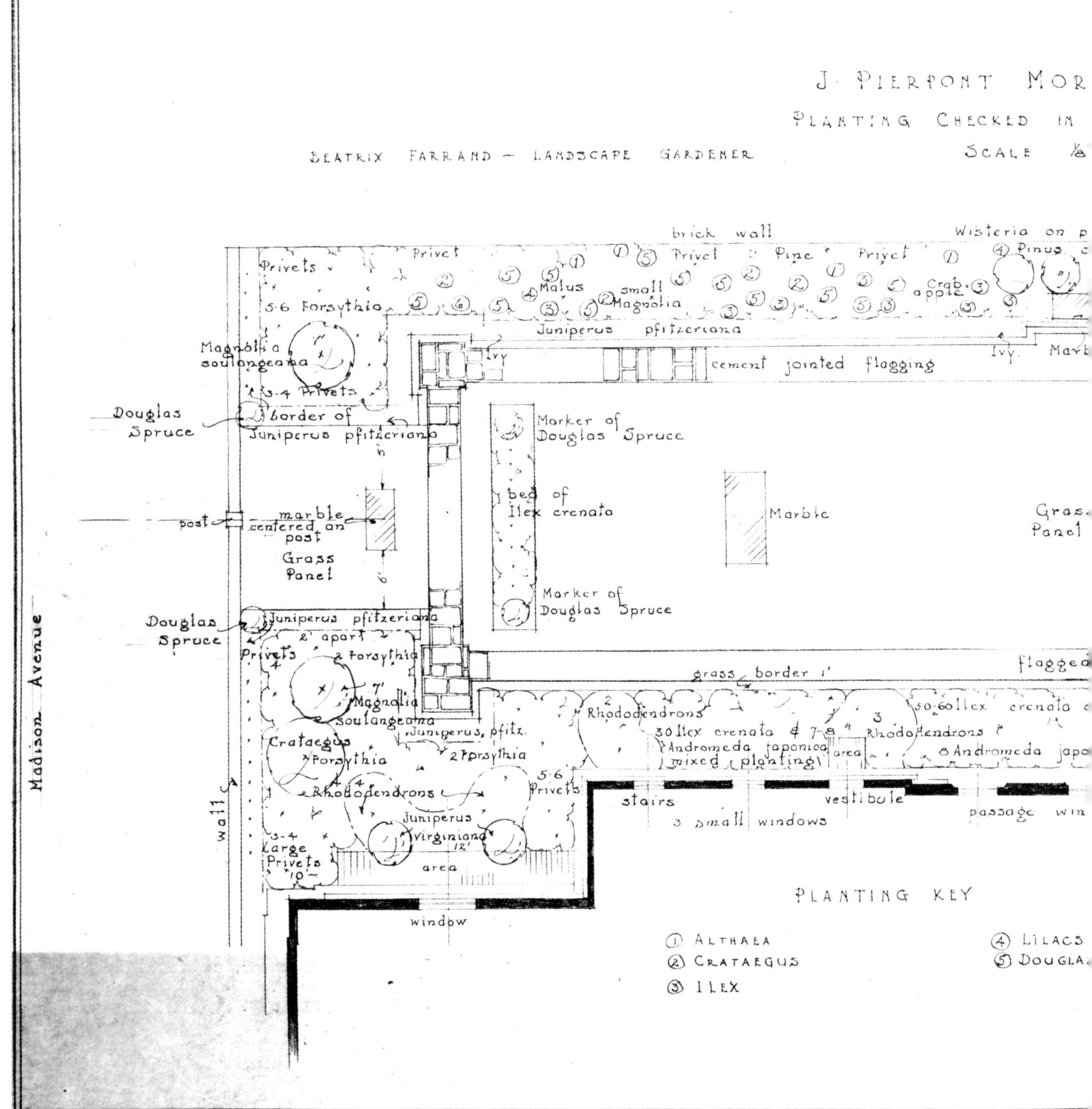

16. Plan for the Pierpont Morgan Library, June 1928. Courtesy of University of California, Berkeley; Department of Landscape Architecture; Documents Collection.

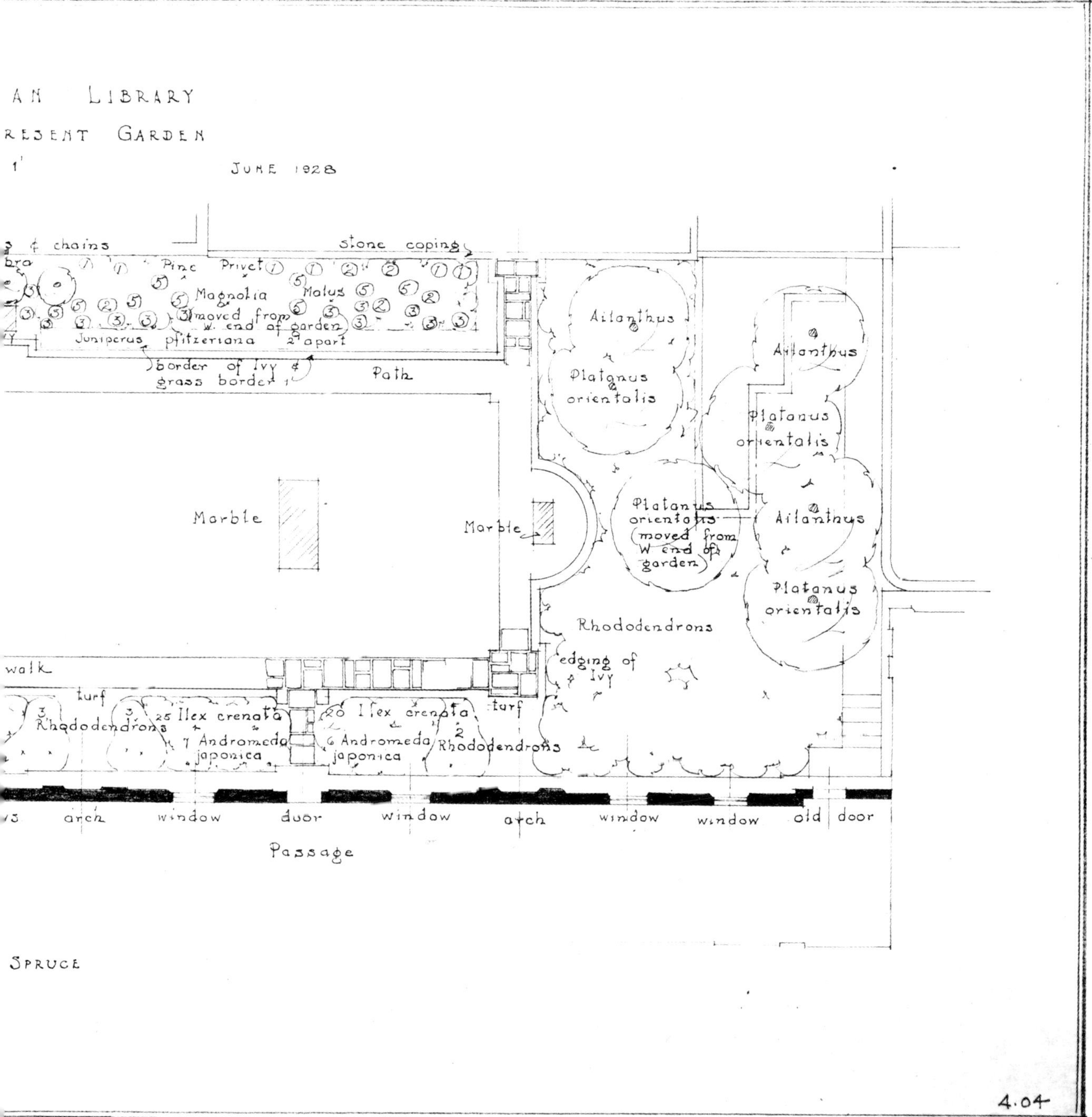

AN LIBRARY
RESENT GARDEN
JUNE 1928
& chains
stone coping
Pine Privet
Magnolia
Malus
moved from W. end of garden
Juniperus pfitzeriana 2' apart
border of Ivy & grass border
Path
Ailanthus
Platanus orientalis
Ailanthus
Platanus orientalis
Platanus orientalis (moved from W end of garden)
Ailanthus
Platanus orientalis
Marble
Marble
Rhododendrons
edging of Ivy
walk
turf
3 Rhododendrons
25 Ilex crenata
7 Andromeda japonica
20 Ilex crenata
6 Andromeda japonica
2 Rhododendrons
turf
arch
window
door
window
arch
window
window
old door
Passage
SPRUCE
4.04

garden was like. Surviving plans dated June 1928 (fig. 16) indicate a long, narrow rectangular panel of grass framed by primarily evergreen material, with occasional flowering trees. Given considerations of economy, much of this material undoubtedly had been retained from the original garden. At the east end was a semicircular terrace. Marble sculptures, now gone, were placed symmetrically at either end of the central panel of grass.

Beyond her role in the design and supervision of the library garden, Farrand now supervised the planting of plane trees adjacent to the property along 36th Street and Madison Avenue. She designed tree guards, argued with the Park Department, and complained when the city recommended the removal of the guards she thought to keep. Writing to J. Axten, Morgan's secretary, she wisely suggested:

> *If the guards surrounding the trees and the gratings over their roots are taken out at present the cost of replacement which must be borne by the owner is $4.65 per tree, for installing the Belgian block which is required by the Park Department. In my opinion it would be better not to make any change in the tree protection for this winter as the cost would amount to a considerable sum.*

Farrand's relationship with the client was cordial over the years but not unmarked by differences of opinion over maintenance costs. Morgan once asked Farrand to lower the weekly salary of one of the gardeners. Still, Morgan sent canisters of Chinese tea each Christmas to the Farrands who reciprocated by sending Portuguese plums. Farrand's long association with the Morgan family came abruptly to an end, however, when shortly after the younger Morgan's death she was fired by the trustees, ostensibly in the interests of economy. Her final letter, addressed to J. Axten and dated 16 August 1943, is touching and typically dignified:

> *Will you please tell the trustees that I shall be glad to help in any way most useful to them as my affection for the garden and the happy relation*

17. Wisteria and post remaining today in the Pierpont Morgan garden, New York City. This section is now the property of the Lutheran Church in America. Photograph: Elizabeth Baumgartner.

with several generations of the Morgan family make me eager to be of as much use as possible.

It is unlikely that I shall be in New York before the first of September. I am therefore enclosing the key to the 37th Street iron gate which was the garden entrance I have used in connection with my inspections.

Sadly, the original library garden has been neglected over the years. The central grass plot is now overgrown with weeds. Only one or two flowering crab trees (planted originally in 1924), several wooden posts, and some remaining wisteria vines survive from Farrand's time (fig. 17).

The Willard Straight Estate, Old Westbury, Long Island (1914–1932)

The estate designed by Farrand for Willard and Dorothy Straight at Old Westbury is representative of a group of large private estates on Long Island which she designed between 1914 and 1932. To this group also belong, among others: Grove Point, for S. Vernon Mann at Great Neck (1918–1930); the Percy R. Pyne estate at Roslyn (1925–1929); and the Otto Kahn estate at Cold Spring Harbor (1919–1928).

Dorothy Payne Whitney, before her marriage to Willard Straight, had traveled widely in Europe. She met Straight, a distinguished international banker and partner of the J. P. Morgan firm, in Washington in 1909. Following a trip around the world which took her to Japan, Korea, China, Hong Kong, Burma, India, and Ceylon, she traveled the following year with Willard Straight and Beatrice Bend in Europe. Dorothy and Willard were married in Geneva, Switzerland in September 1911. At the end of a honeymoon trip that began in Europe and continued, en route to Peking, on the Trans-Siberian Railway, they spent six months in China, on the eve of the Chinese Revolution. Willard Straight maintained intellectual connections in China and the Far East and founded, with Dorothy, *Asia* magazine and, subsequently, the liberal political journal, *The New Republic*. The Straights lived in New York City, at 1130 Fifth Avenue, in a town house designed by Aldrich and Delano (now occupied by the International Center for Photography). Summers were spent at Old Westbury, though Dorothy occasionally took the children to the Adirondacks or to Woods Hole.

Documentary evidence for the Straight estate, which included, beyond the formal Chinese garden, stables and tennis courts, is essentially complete. One hundred twenty drawings, plans, sketches and photographs preserved at the University of California offer a comprehensive picture of the development of this extensive garden.[39]

The plan (pl. II) and perspective views (fig. 18) executed in watercolor (possibly by Farrand's principal assistant, landscape architect Anne Baker) in 1914 are among the most attractive drawings produced by Farrand's office. From the plan, the garden appears to have been situated on a fairly flat plain

18. Perspective view of the Willard Straight estate, Old Westbury, New York, 1914. Courtesy of University of California, Berkeley; Department of Landscape Architecture; Documents Collection.

below the house (also designed by Aldrich and Delano). The approach, through a semicircular forecourt, led to a long, rectangular, grass plot, placed deliberately just off axis with the house. Flanking the central lawn were two parterre flower gardens enclosed by brick wall. Two arbors occupied the central portion of the design. Finally, a swimming pool, framed by lawn, led to two, symmetrically placed pool houses. From the perspective view it is possible to see further details. The approach was flanked by handsome brick piers supporting iron gates. The two middle arbors, constructed in wood, were Chinese in character, reflecting the experience and taste of the clients. The brick wall enclosing the whole was pierced by so-called "moon," or Chinese, gates.

Typically, the original plan was actually carried out over a period of twenty years. Construction details for arbors (fig. 19) and pool houses (fig. 20), as well as other details, were checked and revised again and again by Anne Baker, who corresponded on a weekly basis, from her own New York office at 36 West 11th Street, with Farrand when the latter was in Bar Harbor or elsewhere. A letter from Baker, probably from 1924, is characteristic:

> *The sketch that I am enclosing is of the steps for the Straight playhouse terrace. You said that the terrace was to be of brick laid in right angle herring bone, on sand, and that the steps were to have treads of bluestone with brick risers and brick cheek-blocks. If the cheek-blocks are made of brick that will mean that the top step will have to be brick, too won't it? And that the blue stone of the dry wall will just run against the brick? And, of course the cheek-blocks then will have to be laid up with mortar, or laid*

19. Sketch of the middle arbors for the Willard Straight estate, 1914. Courtesy of University of California, Berkeley; Department of Landscape Architecture; Documents Collection.

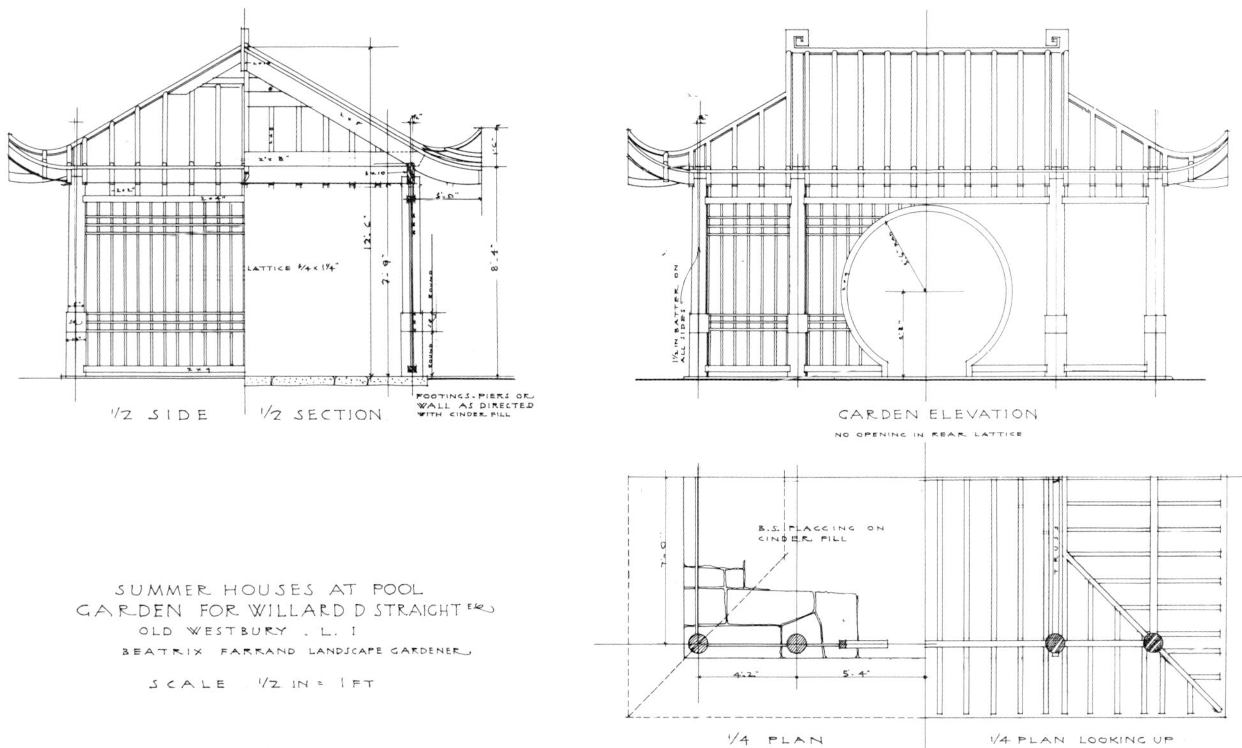

20. Summer houses at the pool of the Willard Straight estate, 1914. Courtesy of University of California, Berkeley; Department of Landscape Architecture; Documents Collection.

> *dry? Of the blue print I sent you, I made the cheek-blocks of stone and I remembered later that you had said you wanted them in brick.*[40]

Another letter indicates that "checking up the garden was a very lengthy process."[41] Baker was in charge, too, of all planting details and was asked in February 1925 to provide a sketch for the railing of the balcony of Dorothy Straight's room, overlooking the gardens.[42]

A photograph of the forecourt to the Chinese garden (fig. 21), as it was called, indicates the quality of the garden as a whole, revealing Farrand's unerring sense for scale and appropriate detail. Planting, paving, and architectural elements—in this case the handsome gate piers crowned by Chinese figures—are carefully combined to give both breadth and intimacy to the space.

21. Forecourt of the Willard Straight garden showing the gate piers. Courtesy of University of California, Berkeley; Department of Landscape Architecture; Documents Collection.

Unfortunately little trace of the Straight garden at Old Westbury remains. Willard Straight died in December 1918. His widow, Dorothy, married Leonard Elmhirst, a Yorkshireman, in 1925 and at that time acquired Dartington Hall in England. Farrand was asked to lay out its grounds and undertake other design work for the gardens—her only commission abroad and one that occupied her intermittently for the remainder of her professional life. Willard and Dorothy's son, Michael, has written that the estate at Westbury was sold and broken into "half acre lots" by a local developer in 1951.[43]

The Abby Aldrich Rockefeller Garden, Seal Harbor, Maine (1926–1950)

Fortunately, we are able to turn to the living work that survives at Seal Harbor and at Dumbarton Oaks in Washington for three-dimensional evidence of Beatrix Farrand's achievement. The Rockefeller garden, like the

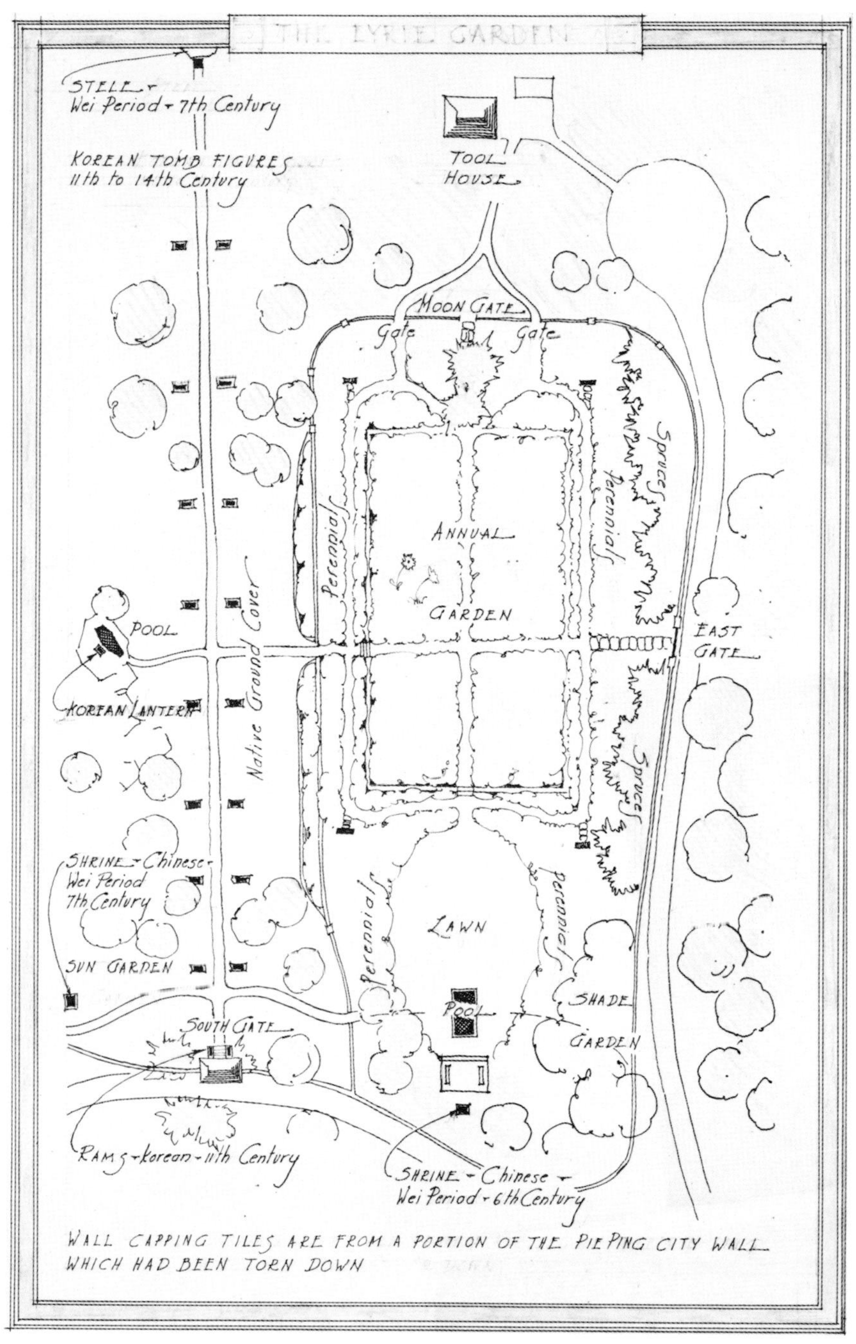

22. General plan of the Eyrie Garden for Abby Aldrich Rockefeller, Seal Harbor, Maine (redesign of the original plan of 1926). Courtesy of University of California, Berkeley; Department of Landscape Architecture; Documents Collection.

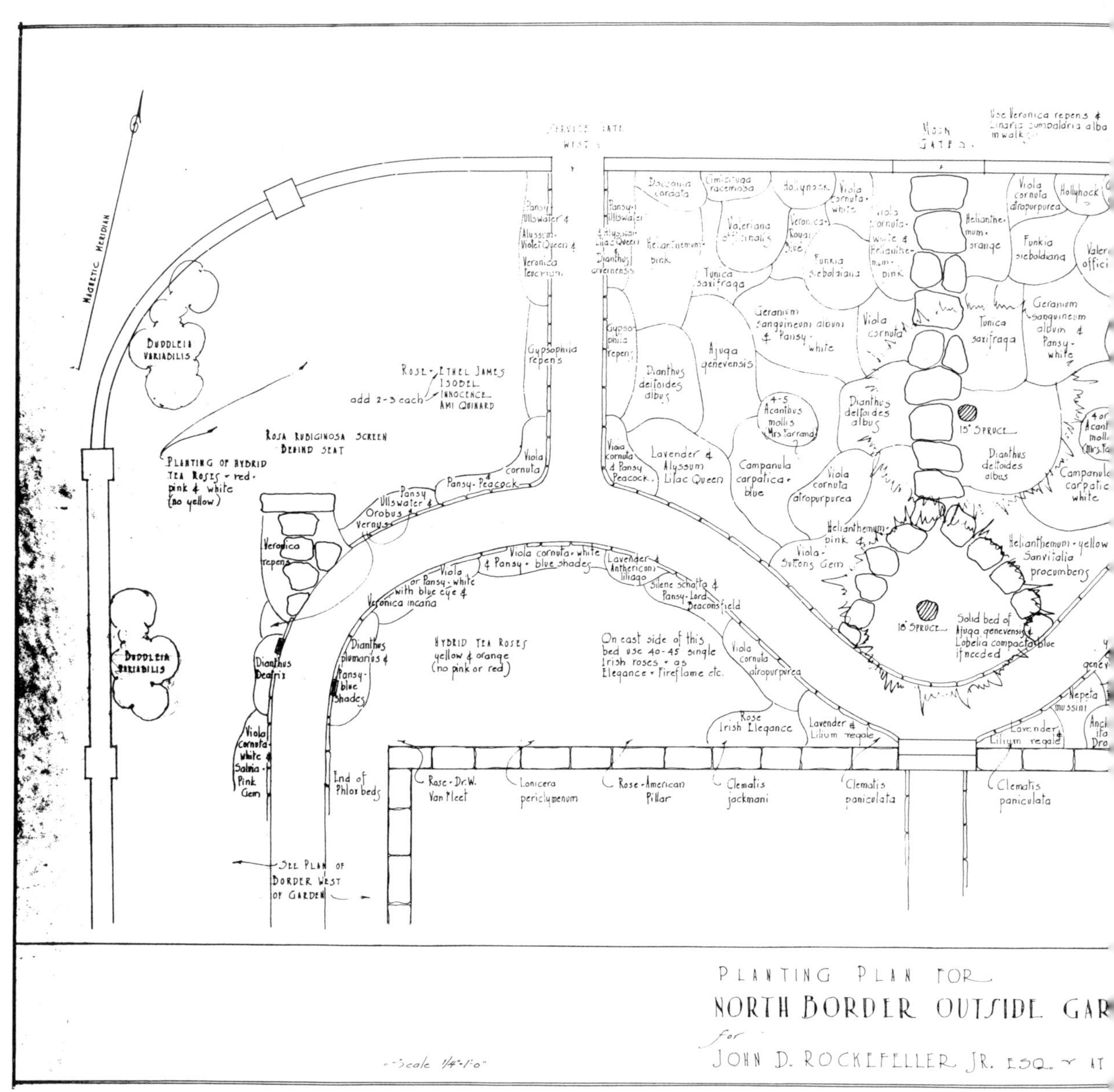

23. Planting plan for the north border of the outside garden at the Rockefeller estate, Seal Harbor, corrected for 1934. Courtesy of University of California, Berkeley; Department of Landscape Architecture; Documents Collection.

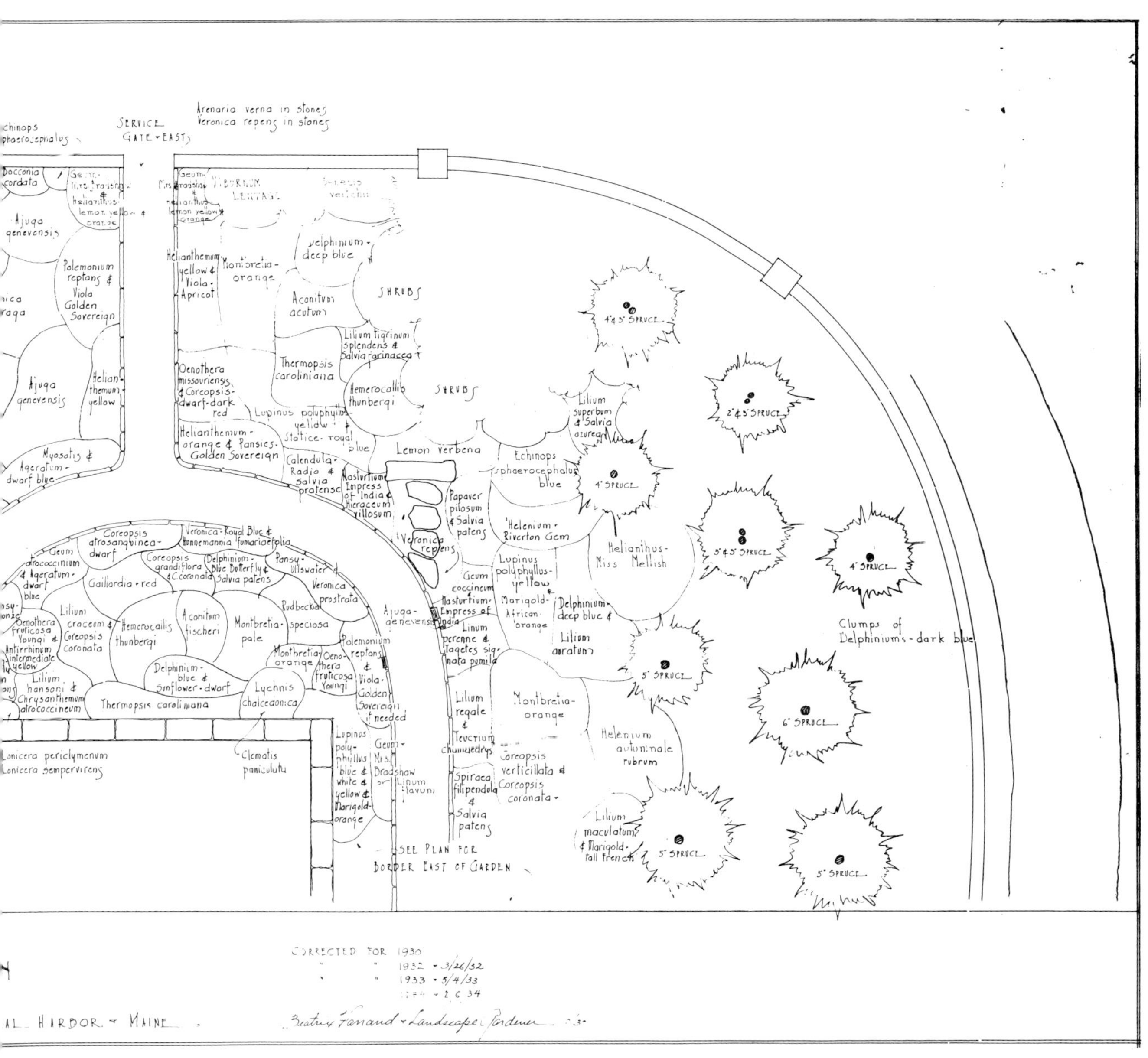

Service Gate - East
Arenaria verna in stones
Veronica repens in stones
Bocconia cordata
Ajuga genevensis
Polemonium reptans & Viola Golden Sovereign
Helianthemum yellow
Myosotis & Ageratum - dwarf blue
Helianthemum yellow & Viola - Apricot
Montbretia - orange
Delphinium - deep blue
Shrubs
Aconitum acutum
Lilium tigrinum splendens & Salvia farinacea
Thermopsis caroliniana
Oenothera missouriensis & Coreopsis - dwarf - dark red
Hemerocallis thunbergi
Lupinus polyphyllus - yellow & Statice - royal blue
Helianthemum - orange & Pansies - Golden Sovereign
Calendula - Radio & Salvia pratense
Nasturtium Empress of India & Hieraceum villosum
Lemon Verbena
Echinops sphaerocephalus blue
Lilium superbum & Salvia azurea
Papaver pilosum & Salvia patens
Veronica repens
Helenium - Riverton Gem
Helianthus - Miss Mellish
Lupinus polyphyllus - yellow
Geum coccineum
Nasturtium - Empress of India
Marigold - African - orange
Delphinium - deep blue &
Lilium auratum
Ajuga - genevensis
Linum perenne & Tagetes signata pumila
Coreopsis atrosanguinea - dwarf
Veronica - Royal Blue & Hunnemannia fumariaefolia
Coreopsis grandiflora & C. coronata
Delphinium - Blue Butterfly & Salvia patens
Pansy - Ullswater &
Veronica prostrata
Gaillardia - red
Lilium croceum & Coreopsis coronata
Hemerocallis thunbergi
Aconitum fischeri
Montbretia - pale
Rudbeckia speciosa
Polemonium reptans & Viola - Golden Sovereign if needed
Montbretia - orange
Oenothera fruticosa Youngi
Delphinium - blue & Sunflower - dwarf
Lychnis chalcedonica
Thermopsis caroliniana
Lilium hansoni & Chrysanthemum atrococcineum
Lilium regale & Teucrium chamaedrys
Montbretia - orange
Helenium autumnale rubrum
Coreopsis verticillata & Coreopsis coronata
Spiraea filipendula & Salvia patens
Lupinus polyphyllus blue & white & yellow & Marigold - orange
Geum - Mrs. Bradshaw & Linum flavum
Lilium maculatum & Marigold - tall French
Lonicera periclymenum
Lonicera sempervirens
Clematis paniculata
See plan for border east of garden
4' & 5' Spruce
2' & 5' Spruce
4' Spruce
5' & 5' Spruce
5' Spruce
6' Spruce
Clumps of Delphiniums - dark blue
Corrected for 1930
" " 1932 - 3/26/32
" " 1933 - 5/4/33
Harbor - Maine
Beatrix Farrand - Landscape Gardener

Straight garden and Dumbarton Oaks, evolved organically over a long period of time. In 1926, Farrand was asked by John D. Rockefeller, Jr., and his wife, Abby, to design the gardens for their summer place, "The Eyrie," at Seal Harbor, Mount Desert Island, Maine. Farrand, who summered (and worked) at her nearby home and experimental garden, Reef Point, had designed several other gardens on Mount Desert Island, including the estate of Herbert Satterlee at Bar Harbor (1921–1939) and "The Haven," for Gerrish H. Milliken at Northeast Harbor (1925–1945). She began her work on the Eyrie Garden in the fall of 1926.

The underlying concept of the garden, shown in the preliminary and subsequent plans (fig. 22), was to provide a secluded setting for Mrs. Rockefeller's collection of oriental sculpture, acquired initially on a trip to the Far East in 1921. A sunken flower garden, enclosed by a high wall and screened by native spruce, pine, maple, birch, and white cedar, provided a foil for the less formal, wooded sculpture garden to the west and to the southwest.

John D. Rockefeller, Jr., wrote to his secretary, C. C. Heydt, in August 1927, reporting that the preliminary site work, the cutting of trees, the removal of stumps, digging of ditches, laying of drain pipes, and initial stone work had been completed.[44] Farrand reported to Rockefeller in October that "the big piece of work done this year" had been to make the planting plans (fig. 23)—"formidable looking documents [which] while as good as I know how to make them, will undoubtedly require occasional alterations as colors of flowers turn out to be not in entire accord with Mrs. Rockefeller's wishes." These planting plans for the annual and perennial gardens were revised almost yearly by Farrand, incorporating Abby Aldrich Rockefeller's recommendations.

By the fall of 1928, the lines for the north and east walls had been clearly established, as had the idea—a pivotal focal-point of the design—of a gate in the north wall. "As the plan seems to work itself out there would be a gate in the surrounding wall on the North," wrote Mrs. Farrand. Outside the gate, and at the top of a few steps, would be a view of the Guardian Figure walk." This was a walk to the west of the sunken garden, lined by Korean figures.

The design of the moon gate (fig. 24) absorbed Farrand's attention for a number of months. She provided full-scale mock-ups or "dummies" (fig.

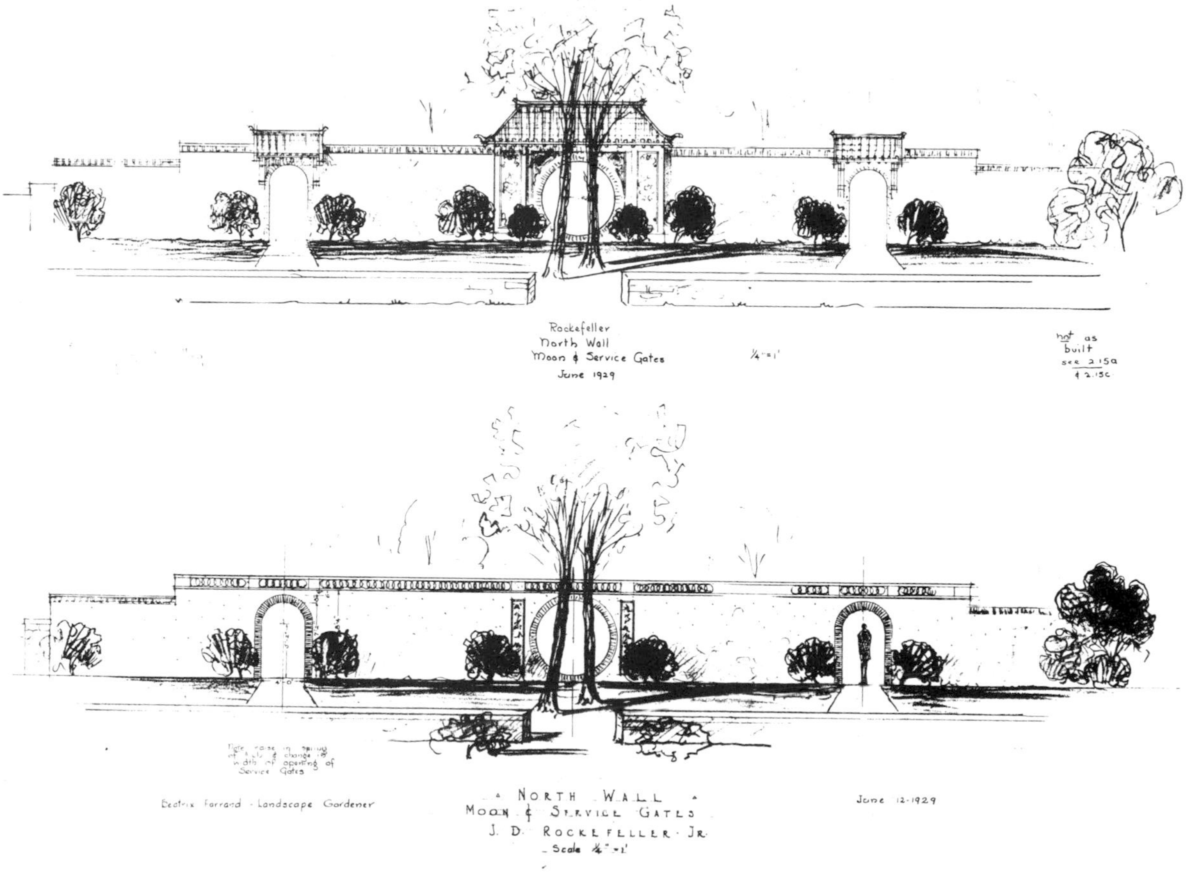

Rockefeller
North Wall
Moon & Service Gates
June 1929

1/4"=1'

not as built
see 2.15a
& 2.15c

Beatrix Farrand - Landscape Gardener

NORTH WALL
MOON & SERVICE GATES
J. D. ROCKEFELLER JR.
Scale 1/4"=1'

June 12-1929

24. Sketch for the north wall, moon and service gates at the Rockefeller estate, Seal Harbor, as built and as not built, 12 June 1929. Courtesy of University of California, Berkeley; Department of Landscape Architecture; Documents Collection.

25. Dummy for the moon gate, the Rockefeller estate, Seal Harbor, 1929. Courtesy of University of California, Berkeley; Department of Landscape Architecture; Documents Collection.

25), as she often did, for several alternative schemes. The final design, deriving from one Mrs. Rockefeller had seen in Peking, went into construction in June 1929. Farrand reported on June 4th:

> *We are . . . boldly and wildly going ahead with the garden work and I have just telegraphed Mrs. Rockefeller to say that unless she tells us to desist we shall go ahead with the north garden wall with its Moon and service gates, stuccoing it in the truly Chinese manner both inside and out. Mr. Candage succeeded in getting a color which to my mind matches the granite shade very attractively.*

What emerges from the lengthy and very detailed correspondence between Farrand and the Rockefellers over the period between 1926 and 1950 is the portrait of a partnership, which continued, not without difficulty, over

26. The Rockefeller estate, Seal Harbor, 1935; the sunken garden is seen beyond the lawn. Courtesy of Rockefeller Archive Center.

27. The Guardian Walk (now called the Spirit Path) at the Rockefeller estate, Seal Harbor, 1960. Photograph: Ezra Stoller.

the years. A letter addressed to Rockefeller, Jr., in 1929 characterizes the design process in general:

> *I am really ashamed to have spent so much time at the Eyrie as I did this last autumn and should not have done so had I not really known that you and Mrs. Rockefeller seemed to want the garden to be quite as perfect a product of our united efforts as possible. Perhaps I have spent more time than was necessary in "mulling" over things, letting the feeling and character of the whole place become a subconscious part of my mind. As you and Mrs. Rockefeller both know, the garden has not been an easy one to design, and if you finally think it successful it will be the result not only of my work but of your own in your constant helpfulness and willingness to discuss its various aspects.*

28. Pool and Korean lantern at the Rockfeller estate, Seal Harbor, 1960. Photograph: Ezra Stoller.

By 1935, the principal elements of the plan—the wall enclosing the garden (crowned by imported Chinese tiles), the sunken flower garden (fig. 26), the moon (pl. III) and bottle gates, the Guardian Walk (fig. 27)—had been completed and other major sculptural elements were in place. Mrs. Rockefeller then decided "to assume full direction of all work in the garden," which she did until 1945 when Farrand was asked to provide ideas for revision of the Chinese Garden, which included the provision of native sod, the installation of new steps along the Guardian Walk, and the extension and

29. The sunken garden at the Rockefeller estate, Seal Harbor, in 1935. Courtesy of the Rockefeller Archive Center.

revision of the sunken flower garden. This work continued under Farrand, with the assistance of Robert Patterson, until the early 1950s.

The garden in its present form, so richly endowed with Korean sculpture, Japanese lanterns, Chinese moon gate, secluded pools (fig. 28) and richly planted flower gardens, retains the basic outlines of the original design. Photographs of the sunken flower garden in 1935 (fig. 29) indicate that it was once more heavily planted. The central portion, now paneled with grass (pl. IV), was much simplified in the early 1960s.

Dumbarton Oaks, Washington, D.C. (1921–1947)

It is to Dumbarton Oaks that the visitor must go for confirmation of Beatrix Farrand's genius as a designer, for it is here that she achieved her finest and most complex work. Working closely with her client, Mildred Bliss, who was herself an imaginative designer, she transformed what formerly had been a farm into one of the finest gardens in this country. Mildred Bliss had always cherished the idea of having a garden of her own throughout her years abroad as the wife of diplomat Robert Woods Bliss. The Blisses purchased a large property in the Georgetown section of Washington, D.C. in 1920, and the gardens evolved under Farrand's direction, beginning in 1921, over the next twenty-six years (fig. 30). The entire composition reflects a

30. Plan of the Dumbarton Oaks gardens, Washington, D.C., in 1941. The Rose Garden (crossed by two east-west walks, one at the foot of a staircase) is at the right, and to its right is the Fountain Terrace. The naturalistic gardens do not appear in the plan as they were no longer a part of the property. Courtesy of Dumbarton Oaks, Trustees for Harvard University.

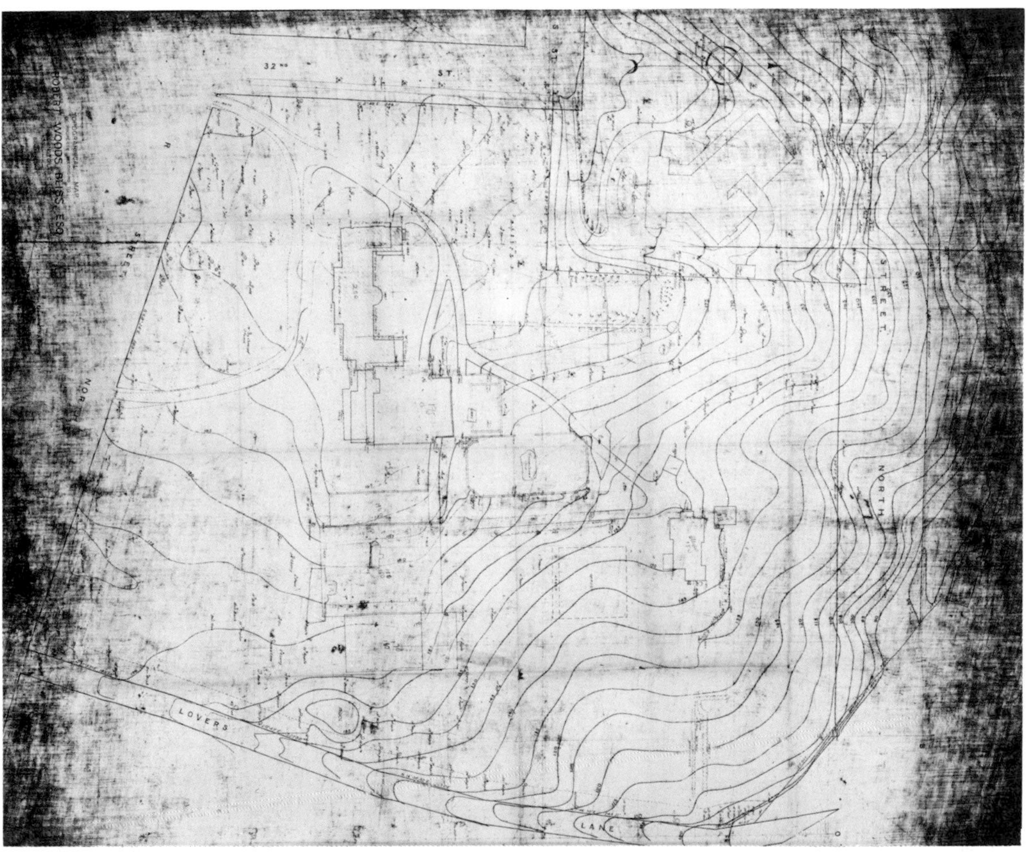

31. Topographic survey of Dumbarton Oaks, 1922. Courtesy of Dumbarton Oaks, Trustees for Harvard University.

clear understanding of the topographic subtleties of the site (fig. 31). "Never did Beatrix Farrand impose on the land an arbitrary concept," wrote Mildred Bliss. She "listened to the light and wind and grade of each area."[45] The gardens are marked by a richness of architectural detail as well as a sense of delicacy and restraint in planting, qualities associated with all Farrand's best work.

Georgina Masson has written perceptively of the principles governing the design of the gardens.[46] Farrand was given the opportunity here to reconcile both formal and informal elements within an overall design. This scheme, given tentative expression in an earlier plan for Edward Whitney, is given total realization here. Gardens nearest the house reflect the formal character of the Georgian manor house (fig. 32). The upper terraces are

32. View of the Green Terrace, Dumbarton Oaks, facing away from the house. Courtesy of Dumbarton Oaks, Trustees for Harvard University.

33. Steps leading from the orangery past the Box Terrace and down into the Rose Garden, Dumbarton Oaks. Courtesy of Dumbarton Oaks, Trustees for Harvard University.

34. Lover's Lane or Mélissande's Allée, Dumbarton Oaks. Courtesy of Dumbarton Oaks, Trustees for Harvard University.

conceived as outdoor rooms for entertaining. The descending series of walled terraces to the east (fig. 33)—the Box (or Urn) Terrace, the Rose Garden, the Fountain Terrace—are conceived separately and experienced individually but always with the idea of there being another garden within view. Orchards, secluded seats, meandering walks (figs. 34 & 35), and informal groups of trees (fig. 36) or shrubs appear at lower levels. Finally there is a naturalistic park (fig. 37) which lies now beyond a gate at the bottom of the steep slope descending from the house to Rock Creek. Rarely is the entire composition understood at once.

Lending complexity to the whole is the principle of asymmetry. As Robert Patterson has said, "Beatrix Farrand's gardens always had a subtle softness of line and an unobtrusive asymmetry. No surface completely flat, no object balanced another of exactly equal weight and position."[47] The house itself, though it commands an impressive north vista, is placed deliberately off axis with the principal terraces extending to the east and descending to the wooded areas below. Often, when resolution is expected, a sudden turn in the walk leads to some unseen arbor, some unanticipated part of the garden.

35. An arbor on the middle slope, Dumbarton Oaks. Courtesy of Dumbarton Oaks, Trustees for Harvard University.

36. Cherry Hill, Dumbarton Oaks. Courtesy of Dumbarton Oaks, Trustees for Harvard University.

37. Stream in the lower, naturalistic garden, Dumbarton Oaks. Courtesy of Dumbarton Oaks, Trustees for Harvard University.

The poetic dimension of the garden, so intricately structured, unfolds gradually, offering moments of revelation. There are aspects of repose and dignity—the Box Terrace or the Beech Terrace. Carefully measured steps descend through box walks to pools of water. There are lyric flights of imagination. Willows sway above the swimming pool, forsythia spirals downward to unseen streams below. There are excursions reminiscent of some garden seen long ago. One of the most evocative places in the garden is the Lover's Lane pool with its charming open-air theatre, an interpretation of the Arcadian Academy in Rome (fig. 38).[48] Here, gracefully sculpted columns and delicate groves of bamboo enclose the dark, oval pool mirroring ancient trees. Finally, there is the descent to the lowest part of the garden, beyond a wooden gate to a stream, a rustic arbor, a stone bridge perhaps reminiscent of Farrand's childhood in Maine. Beatrix Farrand once wrote of the copse north of the Dumbarton Oaks music room that the idea of the planting was "to keep it as poetic . . . as possible," to make it "the sort of place in which thrushes sing and . . . dreams are dreamt."[49]

No other garden in this country has the power to evoke on so many levels, other passages, other moments in time. It is the chambered nautilus of gardens, suggesting at every turn deeper levels of meaning and experience. It is this quality above all others that makes Dumbarton Oaks an enduring work of art.

38. Lover's Lane pool and amphitheatre at the eastern end of the gardens, Dumbarton Oaks. Courtesy of Dumbarton Oaks, Trustees for Harvard University.

39. Stone retaining wall with brick lattice and limestone coping, the Rose Garden, Dumbarton Oaks, 1938; the Box (or Urn) Terrace is at the level above, on the far side of the wall. Courtesy of Dumbarton Oaks, Trustees for Harvard University.

PLANTS AND PLANTING DESIGN

DIANE KOSTIAL McGUIRE

A LATE AFTERNOON IN EARLY FALL, as I was walking through the gardens at Dumbarton Oaks, I came to the Green Terrace, adjacent to the recently renovated orangery, and as I stood in the shade of the great black oak that dominates this hillside and provides a focal point for the terrace, an irate visitor accosted me and asked if she could make a complaint. I must have looked receptive, because she did not hesitate to pour forth her indignation about the fact that having traveled three thousand miles from California to see the gardens at Dumbarton Oaks and having walked through the garden with her friend (who stood rather embarrassed at her side), they had found few flowers. "Where are the flowers? Where are the display gardens? Where is the color?" she asked, looking angrily around the terrace (fig. 40), her eyes fastening on a large terra rosa pot containing a handsome citrus, its foliage clear and green. She fixed on the bare earth at the base of the plant. "Look at that!" she said. "In California, that would be filled with flowers. It would give sparkle and interest to this terrace. There are so many things you could do here to make this a real garden, and I am very disappointed!"

Is it not true in gardening that whenever visitors come, they are always a week too late or two weeks too early for whatever display you wished them to see, and the garden never seems to be quite right? In this case, however, it was not only that plantings were not quite right (the herbaceous border was being changed from summer to fall and the chrysanthemums

40. The north front of the orangery and the Green Terrace, Dumbarton Oaks, in 1938. Courtesy of Dumbarton Oaks, Trustees for Harvard University.

were not yet sufficiently open); there was also a fundamental difficulty of perception on the part of our visitor. In her quest for color, for bright floral display, she had completely overlooked subtle gradations of texture; carefully designed contrasts between light and dark; the thoughtful planning of space, distances, and of progression through the garden. She had been looking solely for color and, more specifically, color provided by flowers. Our visitor eloquently expressed what many people feel: that a true garden is a garden of flowers—that flowers define the meaning of the word "garden." In Beatrix Farrand's garden design, she recognized the importance of flowers, but they were for her only one element that was superseded by the importance of overall design, where each part makes a contribution to the

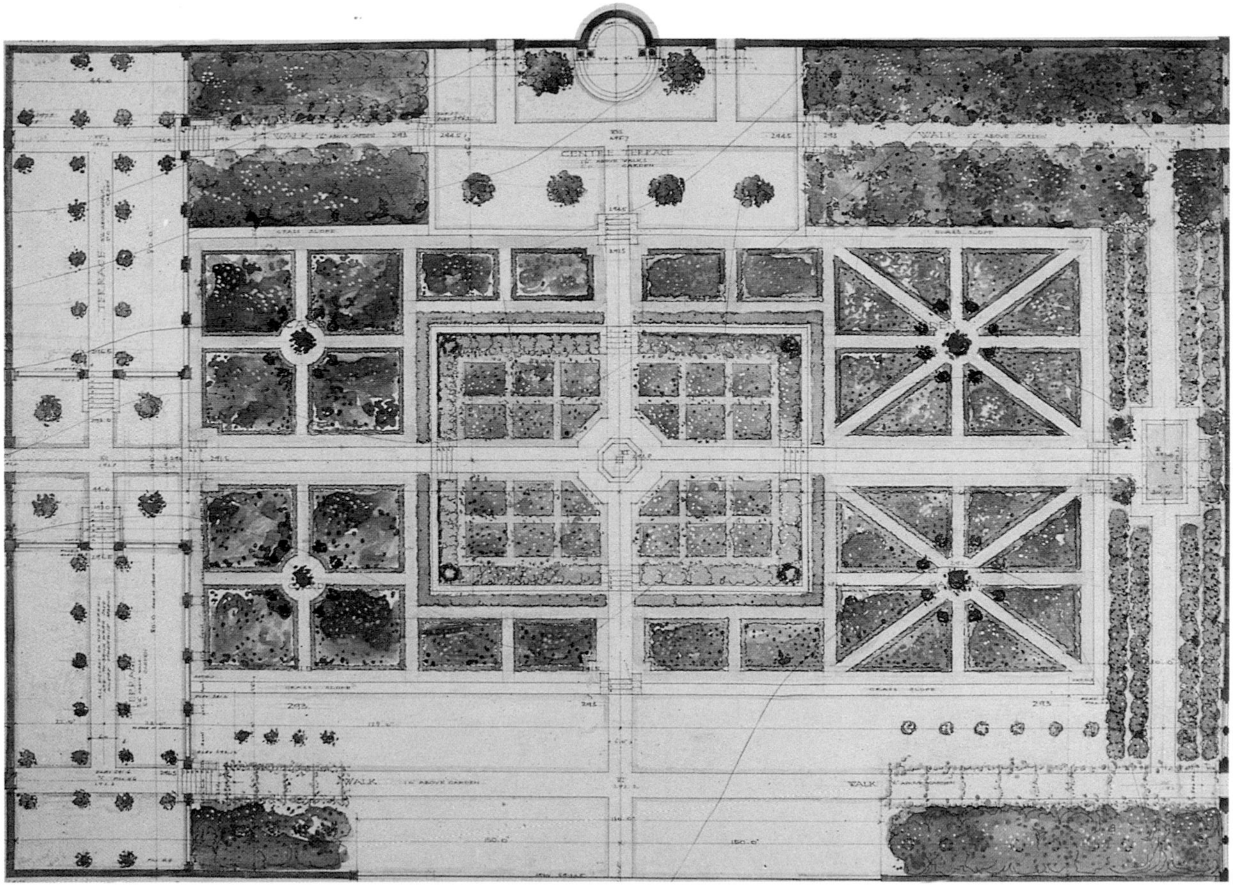

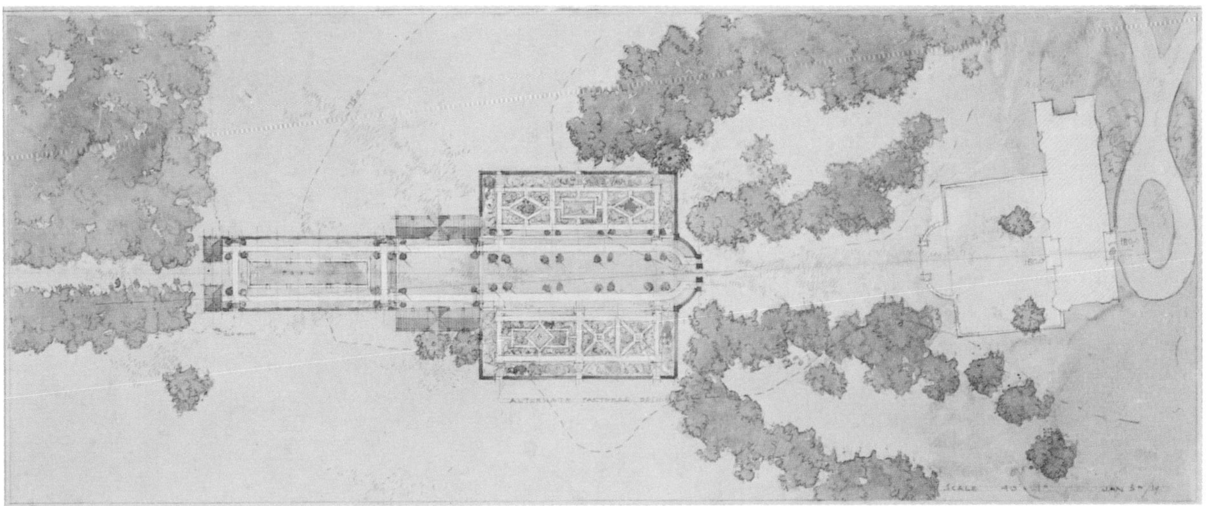

I. Plan for Clement Newbold, Jenkintown, Pennsylvania, about 1901. Courtesy of University of California, Berkeley; Department of Landscape Architecture; Documents Collection.

II. Plan of the Willard Straight estate, Old Westbury, New York, 1914. Courtesy of University of California, Berkeley; Department of Landscape Architecture; Documents Collection.

III. The north border outside the garden at the Rockefeller estate, Seal Harbor, Maine, showing the moon

gate, 1980. Photograph: Alan Ward.

IV. The moon gate at the Rockefeller estate, Seal Harbor, with view into the sunken garden, 1960. Photograph: Alan Ward.

V. The west perennial borders at the Rockefeller estate, Seal Harbor, 1984. Photograph: Alan Ward.

VI. The Forsythia Dell at Dumbarton Oaks with Cherry Hill in the background. Photograph: Ursula Pariser.

VII. South entrance to the Rose Garden, Dumbarton Oaks. Photograph: Ursula Pariser.

VIII. The Rose Garden at Dumbarton Oaks, looking southeast, 1984. Photograph: Cymie R. Payne.

IX. Fall planting of the herbaceous border at Dumbarton Oaks with *Acer platanoides* in the background, 1941. Courtesy of Dumbarton Oaks, Trustees for Harvard University.

X. *Olea europaea* at the Director's House, the Henry E. Huntington Library, San Marino, California. Beatrix Farrand's California studio is in the background. Photograph: Mary Asher.

whole and never upsets the carefully contrived balance. It is this balance in design that gives Farrand's gardens their feeling of repose, tranquility and comfort and makes them so satisfying to visit again and again, at every season of the year.

COLOR IN THE GARDEN

Farrand's use of color in the garden was primarily the result of sophisticated taste, a thorough understanding of texture (how the texture of a material affects the perception of the color of that material), a lifelong study of plant relationships in their natural state, a botanical interest in the detail of plants, and an innate conservatism which resulted in color that was subdued, rich, complex, and always expressive of the essence of the surrounding landscape.

In her use of color she was primarily influenced by Gertrude Jekyll, especially in the planning of herbaceous borders. In her overall planting design she went beyond the limitations of Jekyll's influence; other landscape architects, such as Thomas Mawson (1861–1933), exerted more influence in her lifelong process of self-education. Although Farrand did meet Gertrude Jekyll and did see some of her designs firsthand, the major influence from Jekyll came through the reading and rereading of her books. Beginning with *Wood and Garden,* published in 1899, Farrand continued to add Jekyll's books to her Reef Point collection. Of the greatest influence in her planting design were *Wood and Garden* (1899), *Lilies for English Gardens* (1901), *Wall and Water-Gardens* (1901), and *Colour in the Flower Garden* (1908).

Primarily, Jekyll offered the fundamental idea of painting the garden as would an artist.

> *Whether the arrangement is simple and modest, whether it is bold and gorgeous, whether it is obvious or whether it is subtle, the aim is always to use the plants to the best of one's means and intelligence so as to form pictures of living beauty.*[1]

Plate IX is a color photograph of the herbaceous border at Dumbarton Oaks taken in the early 1940s. The coloring of the border as planned by Beatrix Farrand (and Mildred Bliss, who, with her husband, commissioned the gardens and involved herself in every decision) picks up the brilliance of the Norway maple planted at the terminus and reveals the strong Jekyll influence in color choice and subtle variation.

> *The whole garden was treated in one harmonious colouring of full yellow, orange and orange-brown; half-hardy annuals, such as French and African Marigolds, Zinnias and Nasturtiums, being freely used. It was the most noble treatment of one limited range of colouring I have ever seen in a garden; brilliant without being garish, and sumptuously gorgeous without the reproach of gaudiness—a precious lesson in temperance and restraint in the use of the one colour, and an admirable exposition of its powerful effect in the hands of a true artist.*[2]

Farrand followed Jekyll's advice in the planting of flower borders for various times of the year. Jekyll strongly felt that the flower border could only stay presentable for three months at the most. The herbaceous border at Dumbarton Oaks is still planted in this fashion, according to Farrand's directive, with a spring border, a summer garden, and a fall border. (During the Blisses' lifetimes, the emphasis was only on spring and fall as they were not in residence during the summer months.) On the other hand, in the many gardens Farrand planned on Mount Desert Island—the most famous is the Abby Aldrich Rockefeller Garden in Seal Harbor which is still maintained according to the original plan—the herbaceous borders were for summer only. At the Rockefeller garden, for a brief two months can still be seen her "sumptuously gorgeous" colors, used with "temperance and restraint" (pl. V). These flower beds are probably the closest thing we have in America to the grandeur and subtlety of the Gertrude Jekyll herbaceous border.

Farrand and Jekyll had many attitudes in common, which resulted in similarities of approach regarding color, but there were significant differences which characterize each of these women as an artist. Jekyll's work was primarily concerned with the flower garden and with flowers as they appeared in the broader landscape. When she speaks of color in the garden, it is the color of flowers. Farrand concerned herself with the color of foliage to a much greater extent. Jekyll was not a designer or architect of gardens in the manner that Farrand was. Many of the important Jekyll gardens were designed in collaboration with the architect Edwin Lutyens. He was responsible for the general layout—the structure—she for the choice of plants, primarily the flower borders. (Similarly, Vita Sackville-West's famous garden at Sissinghurst, which also echoes many Jekyll principles, especially in combinations of plants, was designed in the overall sense by Harold Nicholson. He has not been given sufficient recognition for his vitally important role in the success of that garden.) Beatrix Farrand, on the other hand, was both garden designer and plantswoman. She considered that one of the cardinal rules in the development of any property was to pay close attention to the land and to let the land dictate the form of the garden. This necessitates that the designer be thoroughly familiar with the site, which means many visits and a willingness not to impose preconceived ideas on the land. Gertrude Jekyll rarely made site visits, and almost all of her later designs were drawn without firsthand knowledge of special site problems or of the unique opportunities they presented. Also in contrast to Jekyll, Farrand conceived of color in the garden as extending far beyond the confines of the herbaceous border. Rather, she concerned herself with the entire property as a single visual entity and included leaf color and fruit in her planning, as well as the more obvious relationships of flowers.

Although Farrand had no prolonged formal education in art, she was diligent in reading, study, and observation of plant color, both as it occurred in nature and in deliberate garden groupings. She closely examined Jekyll's plans, and because of her own extensive travels in England she was familiar with how Jekyll's plants grew in the English climate and how they differed in appearance in American gardens. She was also painfully aware of the vast discrepancy in standards of maintenance between English and American gardens. When she had to give up her long-cherished dream of Reef Point as a place of study for horticulturists and garden designers (fig. 41), she ruefully remarked that it had become clear that the inhabitants of the region did not have horticultural sap running in their veins, as did the inhabitants of Britain.

It was one of the great pleasures of Farrand's later gardening life that she was able, in 1948, to purchase from the Massachusetts Horticultural Society Gertrude Jekyll's garden plans, working drawings, and accompanying correspondence. The papers had been given during World War II by Jekyll's nephew to the Royal Horticultural Society as his contribution toward their Red Cross sale fund and they constituted practically the entire inventory of her work. At the time of the purchase, Farrand hoped that her gardens and library at Reef Point would ultimately become an institution for the study of plants and garden design. Doubtless, she bought the collection with that in mind, but it also enabled her to make a firsthand examination of the work of this famous landscape gardener whom she had so admired and in many ways emulated. Beatrix Farrand was seventy-six at the time of the purchase, and though she was still working on a number of projects—most notably the Santa Barbara Botanic Garden (pl. XV) where she was Chief

41. The major plant groupings at Reef Point Gardens, Bar Harbor, Maine (from the *Reef Point Gardens Bulletin,* June 1956).

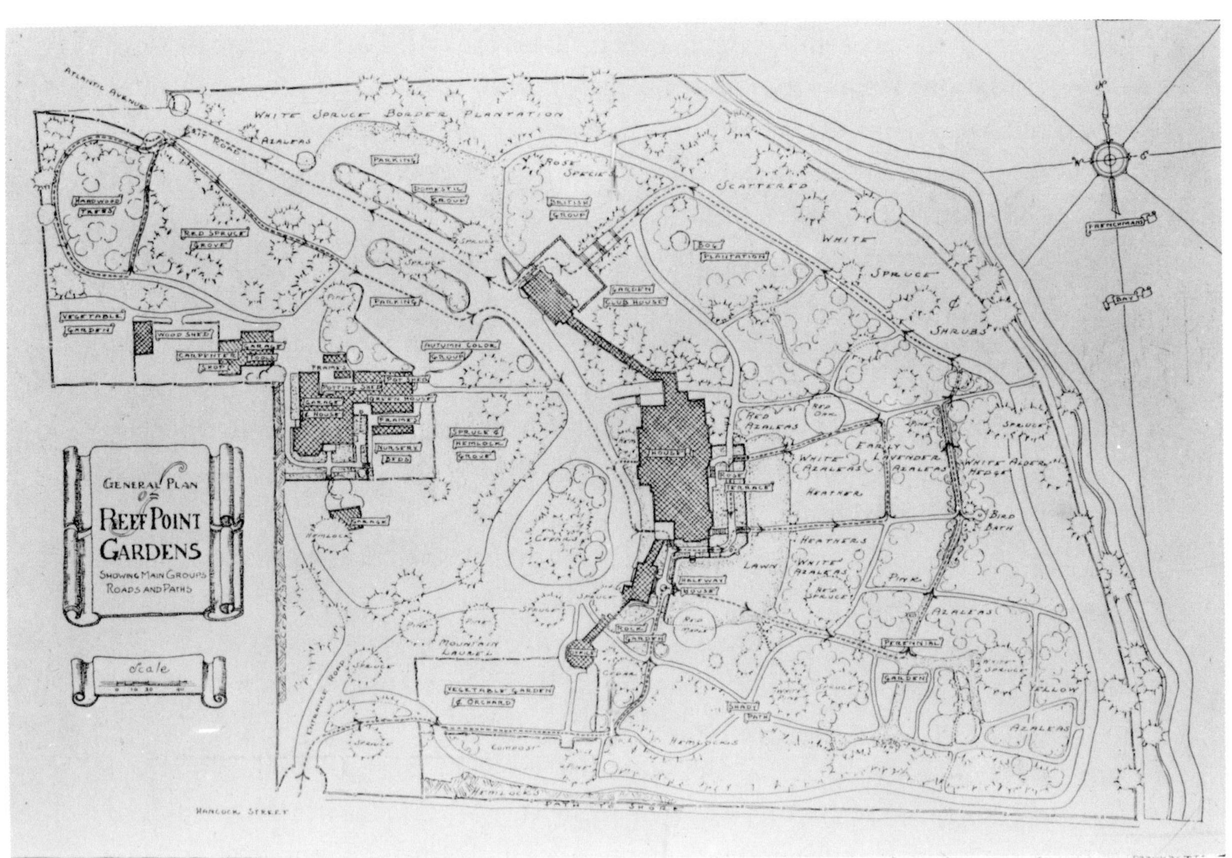

Consultant for Planning and Landscape Gardening—the major gardens of her fifty-year career had been completed. The Jekyll papers came too late to be applied to her own designs, but they brought her much pleasure. She was able to study them in depth, which she greatly appreciated, having not had the leisure when her professional life was at its peak of activity. If she learned anything from them that she had not absorbed from her earliest reading of Jekyll's books, she had no opportunity at this late stage to apply the lesson. And, unfortunately, she left no written account of her research. Indeed, in contrast to Jekyll, she wrote very little during her lifetime. What we know of Beatrix Farrand's taste in color—of her taste in all aspects of garden design—comes primarily from studying her extant gardens, her surviving garden plans, and the reports and correspondence relating to them.

Color in the garden is emphatically a matter of personal taste, surely the most individualized aspect of gardening and one easily altered by intervention from another individual. It presents one of the greatest difficulties in the accurate presentation of older gardens to the public, where the distribution of responsibility over many years has taken many decisions out of the hands of the original designer and placed them in those of the resident gardener. Gardeners, by nature, are prone to the uninhibited expression of horticultural enthusiasm and are generally uninterested in historical accuracy or in achieving the authentic expression of someone else's taste. The floral palette at Dumbarton Oaks today and in the Abby Aldrich Rockefeller Garden is not precisely as it was when Beatrix Farrand was compiling yearly lists. This is not due to lack of historical documentation but to a combination of the absence of the original designer with other factors. Tastes change. Colors fall in and out of favor. And plant "improvement" renders earlier forms obsolete, substituting doubles for singles; frills and scallops for simpler edges; and larger size with an attending lack of fragrance for delicacy in scale and subtle scents.

The Rose Garden at Dumbarton Oaks (pl. VIII) is the best extant example of a garden expressing Farrand's ideas on color and the type of planting she considered appropriate for formal gardens; yet this garden is still in a transitional stage of restoration and it will be a few more years before the effect she desired is again achieved. When the gardens as a whole were in their initial planning stage in 1921, it was decided by Mildred Bliss and

Beatrix Farrand that the terracing of the major hillside to the east would contain a rose garden and that this rose garden would be the principal feature. Considering the gardens at Dumbarton Oaks as a series of "rooms," as did their designer, the Rose Garden dominates. It is the grand ballroom.

The Rose Garden is a large flat plane (123′4″ north-to-south by 88′6″ east-to-west). Above the garden to the west, separated from it by a high stone retaining wall (10′4″, including an open brick-work balustrade; fig. 39) is the Box (or Urn) Terrace (figs. 42 & 43), intended to provide an overlook into the Rose Garden and therefore designed in contrast to it with an atmosphere of calmness and repose, without excitement in color, in order to prepare one for the visual interest below. The two terraces complement one another.

Below the Rose Garden is the Fountain Terrace, not directly visible because of Farrand's introduction of a double staircase leading to this lower elevation. In her plan, both the east and west boundaries of the Rose Garden serve to give it contained form, on the one side, the Box Terrace wall providing a backdrop for the display of climbing plants, and on the other a strong edge which forms a boundary to the rose display. To the north, the garden wall is partially retaining and partially free-standing. Its most important features are the gate piers, the gate, and the overthrow. The piers are fashioned of brick, which contrasts with the stone walls. The piers and gate are repeated on the south side of the garden (pl. VII), thereby introducing a north-south axis. This axis is secondary to that leading between the Box and Fountain Terraces, and yet is of importance because it proposes the possibility of north-south movement into and out of the garden, thereby expanding the space in the same manner in which a wall appears to change the dimensions of a room when it is punctuated by an opening.

The primary structural plantings of the Rose Garden are *Buxus sempervirens* 'Suffruticosa' and *Buxus sempervirens*. The combination of boxwood and lawn on the horizontal plane provides a constant green background which not only enhances the color of the roses but makes the garden beautiful and interesting in midwinter. In 1983, when the fall season in Washington extended into December with relatively warm temperatures until Christmas, the roses, which had been partially frosted, continued to keep their color in bud and acquired an antique look against this deep, almost blue-green back-

42. The northeast corner of the Box (or Urn) Terrace, Dumbarton Oaks, probably in the 1930s. Courtesy of Dumbarton Oaks, Trustees for Harvard University.

43. Brick retaining wall with wall plantings and Japanese anemone on the Box (or Urn) Terrace, Dumbarton Oaks. Courtesy of Dumbarton Oaks, Trustees for Harvard University.

drop. It was as if an illuminated manuscript had come to life in three dimensions.

The boxwood, with its refined texture and modeled effect (due to careful, sensitive pruning) assumes many forms in this garden, all of which work together to unify the whole. Primarily, it provides strong contrast and lends form for the display of the tea roses. The color of the roses, particularly the reds, appears more intense against this sympathetic background, and the flat, blue-green color and coarser texture of the rose foliage contrast with the fineness of the box. Against the high west wall the boxwood is encouraged to grow in more exuberant forms, serving to soften the architecture and to frame the display of climbing roses, which are allowed to intermingle there in a fountain-like, cascading tangle, in contrast to the formal restraint shown in the planting of the patterned beds below.

Although Beatrix Farrand wrote very little on the subject of garden design, she did prepare an extensive report on the Dumbarton Oaks gardens for the benefit of Harvard University at the time the gardens (along with the house and research collections) were given over to that institution. In that report, discovered years later in the files at Dumbarton Oaks and published in 1980 under the title *Beatrix Farrand's Plant Book for Dumbarton Oaks,* she described her conception of the landscaping of the property as a whole and of each distinct garden within it. For each part of the garden, she listed the plants she had chosen and specified the way they should be placed and maintained. Her words on the Rose Garden[3] tell us generally about the color effect she hoped to achieve, but the greater emphasis placed in her text on how the roses were to be displayed is indicative of her architectural approach to gardening:

The Rose Garden

This is the largest of the terraces in the Dumbarton Oaks garden plan. As the gardens were always thought likely to be much seen in winter, the thought behind the planting of the Rose Garden has been given quite as much to the evergreen and enduring outlines and form as to the Roses, which, at their season, give added charm to this level. The Roses in the Rose Garden are really only secondary to the general design of the garden and its form and mass. The high wall, on the west side with its latticed-brick balustrade . . . is an admirable place on which to grow certain climbing Roses, perhaps a Magnolia grandiflora, Clematis paniculata, *and a wispy veil of* Forsythia suspensa *narrowing the steps leading [down] from the Box to the Rose Garden Terrace.*

Big accent Box are used at the entrance steps, and there should be one large clipped Box in the middle of the garden, and probably four more large ones in two each of the north and south beds. These tall Box are intended for winter accent and as foils to the Roses growing alongside them. It is recognized that they are bad neighbors to the Roses, but this disadvantage must be taken into account when the general effect of the year is considered as a whole. Accent Box are also needed in comparatively small size at both the north and the south gates, and at the opening of the steps on the east side of the Garden leading toward the Fountain Terrace.

*The edgings to the Rose beds should also be of Box—*suffruticosa *of varying heights—and no bed border should be allowed to grow too tall. If the Box borders to the beds are allowed to grow too large, the whole terrace becomes dwarfed and becomes a series of Box-enclosed and almost invisible beds. Therefore, the Box edgings must be replaced, perhaps over fifteen or twenty years.*

The center plant in the garden may be allowed to grow to a considerable height, perhaps even fifteen feet, but the designer feels that the marker plants should be distinctly secondary in size, in order not to overwhelm the iron gates at the north and south entrances to the garden or to so dominate the garden that the Roses are hardly noticed.

In choosing the colors for the Roses in general, the pink and salmon color-sorts have been selected for the south third, together with a few of the very deep red ones, such as Etoile de Hollande and Ami Quinard. The center third of the garden was planted more particularly with salmon-colored and yellowish pink Roses, while the northern third was given over entirely to yellow or predominantly yellow and orange sorts.

The beds surrounding these center, formal beds have been used for small, bush Roses, such as the polyantha, *some of the hybrid singles, and some of the smaller species Roses. The climbing Roses grown on the west wall have included Mermaid, Silver Moon, Dr. Van Fleet, American Pillar, Reveil Dijonnais, and Cl. Frau Karl Druschki.*

In every large landscape designed by Beatrix Farrand, the elements of the formal and informal in planting are found. They are also found in the many smaller parts of the whole. This contrast on all levels of scale creates a dynamic tension that underlies the dominating feeling of repose and gives vitality. In the Rose Garden, the plants assume various forms. Some, like the box or like the roses grown along the coping of walls, are extremely controlled; others, like the tea roses, are contained; while the climbers animate the whole with their brilliance of color and vivacity of movement.

The Rose Garden is a formal garden, one of an interlocking series leading from west to east; but from the other side of its walls at the north and south a more informal planting overhangs, becoming a part of the garden by assertion. A grovette of *Cornus florida* grows in a natural form outside the southeast corner, cloaking this corner with delightful leaf-color in fall and delicate white blossoms in spring. Just outside the south gate is an *Ilex opaca* which forms a background for the graceful boxwood inside the gates. Together, the informal and formal elements combine to satisfy the disparate parts of our natures and constantly refresh the eye.

FORMALITY AND INFORMALITY IN THE GARDEN

Thomas Mawson, in his classic book *The Art and Craft of Garden Making* (1900), uses the term "naturalesque" when referring to those more remote parts of a garden to which one has been carefully led, through a series of contrivances which endeavor to give a feeling of natural progression, reversing the journey to civilization. The ideal garden as described by Mawson begins in the mind:

> *First of all to store the mind with the character and style of the house, to make a mental delineation of the outline and mass of its unvarying proportions, then to give connection to, and coherence with the immediate surroundings, securing if possible certain associating links of similarity alike in both house and terrace, or the plateau which is the special domain of the house, then gradually—if the character of the surroundings justify it—lead to the freer and more natural landscape.*[4]

44. *Ulmus americana* planted by Beatrix Farrand in the R Street border at Dumbarton Oaks, 1979. Photograph: Ursula Pariser.

This progression allowed architectural sensibility to reclaim its place in garden design after its eighteenth- and nineteenth-century banishment while at the same time encouraging a more natural landscape to crowd up to the garden walls, providing contrast and interest with planting of a very different sort. Beatrix Farrand followed this path in her work, and many of her gardens are laid out "according to Mawson." In all of her planting schemes, Farrand gave each part of the garden a character appropriate within this progression of decreasing formality away from the house. She did not use wild plants within walls, nor showy hybrids in the naturalistic parts of a garden outside them. There is a logic and balance to her schemes which does not depend on the size of the property. In her smallest gardens, such as the one she created for herself at the Garland Farm on Mount Desert Island, the elements of the naturalistic are ever present on the fringes, although the geometric design of the many flower beds is formal and they are formally planted with different varieties and colors for each bed.

It was at the turn of the century that horticulturists and landscape designers began to turn back from the frenzied interest in exotics that had characterized so much of nineteenth-century landscape design and to look with a new eye and a great deal of affection at what Mawson called "the advocacy of the old hedge-rows, the preference for homely native trees as oak, ash, elm (fig. 44), beech, sycamore, chestnut, holly, yew and box."[5] Gertrude Jekyll, in *Wood and Garden,* advocated this same simplicity. "To devise these living pictures from simple well-known flowers seems to me the best thing to do in gardening."[6]

This return to rusticity on the part of garden designers allowed them to work with materials with which they were familiar. It called upon their knowledge of the landscape of hedgerow and moorland, bringing into the garden plants which they found in the natural world immediately around them and which also had a tradition of local use behind them. Designers turned away from artificiality, from experimentation. Even the serpentine line began to straighten. The kitchen garden continued to be important. There was a revival in the use of many old materials and objects for the garden. Sundials were in demand, and old forms in wood furniture and tubs were revived. Lead statues became of great interest, and large cisterns of lead were built again.

In *The English House,* Herman Muthesius describes how the Englishman crept into the countryside, almost burrowing into the heart of nature:

> *The English house lies in the midst of flower-gardens, facing far away from the street, looking on to broad green lawns which radiate the energy and peace of nature; the house lies long and low, a shelter and a refuge rather than an essay in pomp and architectonic virtuosity; it lies hidden somewhere in the green countryside remote from any center of culture . . . and the house itself, with its cheerful colors and solid forms, fitting so admirably into the surrounding country stands as a witness to the sound instincts of a people, which for all its wealth and advanced civilization, has retained a remarkably strong feeling for nature.*[7]

45. The garden as a series of rooms; looking northward across the herbaceous border, Dumbarton Oaks, 1938. Courtesy of Dumbarton Oaks, Trustees for Harvard University.

46. Reef Point, Bar Harbor, Maine, about 1942. Courtesy of University of California, Berkeley; Department of Landscape Architecture; Documents Collection.

The garden was seen as an extension of the rooms of the house, each "room" having a particular function, such as the display of a particular type of plant or object. The limits of the rooms were clearly delineated by clipped hedges (fig. 45) or walls of stone, brick, or some combination of materials.

Such gardens generally have three essential elements: terraces, flower beds, and lawns; and these elements were usually present in Farrand's most formal, wall-enclosed gardens. Beyond the walled areas she would gradually carry the visitor out through less formal, but nonetheless carefully planned, gardens of various descriptions. These would, as a rule, incorporate indigenous plants, but beyond that one cannot generalize as to their character. She took her cue from the surroundings. At the furthest edge of the property—as at Dumbarton Oaks, where she was attempting to create a country atmosphere within a city, or at Reef Point, at water's edge (fig. 46)—she created a naturalistic landscape that appeared to have been discovered, rather than designed. This progression from formal through informal to naturalistic garden can still be seen at Dumbarton Oaks, although the naturalistic garden has become so overgrown that it is difficult to recognize Farrand's influence there.

Representative of the formal garden is her Fountain Terrace at Dumbarton Oaks. Within this walled enclosure she placed seasonal flower borders, shrub plantings, a considerable number of wall plants, grass walks, and two fountains which Farrand specified should be allowed to become "as mossy as possible. . . . The fountains should appear to have been 'found' there and to be part of the old plan."[8] She may well have intended, through this effect of a "found" element in an otherwise clearly contrived design, to create a transition between the Fountain Terrace and the pastoral landscape not far beyond it. The Fountain Terrace is the last of the formal gardens on the eastern slope, farthest from the house, and it opens out onto a heavily shaded pool with a naturalistic landscape on its far side. The Fountain Terrace (fig. 47), although an enclosed garden, is certainly less formal in effect than the Rose Garden immediately above it.

Farrand's description[9] again indicates the range of her formal-garden designs:

The Fountain Terrace

This terrace is the one real flower garden in the series of terraces sloping eastward from the main building. In the spring, probably the best bulbs to use will be Tulips, in such colors as may be found attractive. The cheapest groups which can be bought in large quantities are those of the mixed Darwins, preferably running toward the yellows, bronzes, and oranges, but if these colors prove difficult to find, the old-fashioned rainbow mixture of all sorts of colors can wisely be susbstituted. It should be insisted that the tulips be supplied of sorts approximately of even height, and all of late-blooming varieties, as "misses" in the border where early-flowering Tulips come and go before the rest of the plantations are in bloom, make decided blanks in the composition. Under

47. The Fountain Terrace at Dumbarton Oaks, looking northward. Courtesy of Dumbarton Oaks, Trustees for Harvard University.

the Tulips, and making a border for them, annuals such as Forget-me-not, Pansies, Daisies, and possibly Arabis, *may be set out. This garden is the one in which most change and replacement is necessary, in order to keep up the blooming effect throughout the season, and any alteration in the scheme permitting this blooming effect throughout the season would seem a mistaken economy. The area planted to the revolving series of flowers is a comparatively small one, and therefore not much space is required for propagation. After the Tulips have finished their blooming, summer-flowering annuals are planted in the borders; in the past, yellows, bronzes, blues, and primrose shades have been found attractive, rather than shades of pink, lavender, or crimson. The autumn display on this terrace, for the last years, has been an effective grouping of yellow Chrysanthemums in various shades, with bronze, deep brown, and maroon, but no pinks or whites have worked in well with this scheme of color. . . .*

The wall on the west side of the Fountain Terrace . . . reveals the sharp drop in level between the Rose Garden and the level of the terrace itself. Here . . . the steps have been broken into three different flights in order to make the climbing not too laborious a process. Two-thirds of the way down the steps, a seat, under a lead canopy, is placed on the landing, and, when possible, is surrounded by pot plants which harmonize in color with those used in the garden.

Outside the east wall of the Fountain Terrace, Kieffer Pear trees are planted in an almost solid hedge that also stretches along the north wall. This hedge is . . . planted as a support to the garden, which otherwise would be obviously hanging over retreating grades and suspended unpleasantly in the air. The great beauty of the planting outside the east wall is a magnificent English Beech (Fagus sylvatica Riversii) *of the darkest shade. Under this, a group of spring-flowering bulbs used to be planted—such as* Leucojum aestivum, *Aconite, and* Scilla nutans *in its different shades—and later-flowering* Tiarella *and some Maidenhair and other ferns. . . . A plant or two of Clematis, Ivy, and fine-leaved* Parthenocissus Lowii *clothe the wall but do not cover it completely.*

On the west wall, on either side of the big flight of steps, Parthenocissus heterophylla *should be allowed to cover this area, and to cover the heavy wall enclosing the steps, as this wall, if unclothed, is overmassive in its scale.*

Two espaliered Magnolia grandiflora *may be used, if not too large, in matching positions on the east side of the west wall; and two fine plants of* Taxus cuspidata *should also be used at the back of the west borders, both to clothe and hide the heavy wall and to reduce the size of the border.*

48. The old Boxwood Ellipse in the northeast section of the gardens at Dumbarton Oaks. Courtesy of Dumbarton Oaks, Trustees for Harvard University.

Outside the terrace on the southwest, a group of flowering Dogwood (Cornus florida) *should be kept constantly replaced, as this feature tends to offset what is again a difficult alteration in level, and to give interest and flower in spring as well as fruit and color in autumn.*

The south gate in the new, south, stone wall is marked by clipped plants of American Holly (Ilex opaca) *at either side. These should not be allowed to become too large, as the garden is of such small size that a heavy pair of plants would throw it out of balance. The south walk is aimed almost immediately at an Apple tree which has been doctored and fed to keep it in good condition. When it fails, it should be replaced by a fair-size tree, as the effect of the rounded top and the blossomed branches, as seen from the south side of the Fountain Terrace, is a valuable part of the composition.*

The transition from the brick walks of the Beech Terrace [the terrace nearest the house] *to the flagged walks of the Rose Garden and again to the grass walks of*

49. Lover's Lane pool at Dumbarton Oaks, 1938. Courtesy of Dumbarton Oaks, Trustees for Harvard University.

the Fountain Terrace has all been carefully thought out, and, as there is no "gangway" either from east to west or from north to south on this terrace, it should be possible to keep the turf in good condition. Two fountains are kept filled and playing during the summer season, and it is important that their curbs be allowed to become as mossy as possible, as, scrubbed and cleaned well, the curbs would look new and fresh and garish, whereas the fountains should appear to have been "found" there and to be a part of the old plan.

In contrast to her formal gardens are Farrand's informal gardens (figs. 48 & 49), less precisely arranged but still definable. The Forsythia Dell at Dumbarton Oaks is a famous example. This dell, of yellow brilliance in spring, represents Jekyll's advice concerning "the inestimable value of the quality called 'breadth' in planting."[10]

50. The Star Garden at Dumbarton Oaks, with informal planting of trees beyond the wall. Courtesy of Dumbarton Oaks, Trustees for Harvard University.

Simplicity of intention and directness of purpose were the major qualities in Farrand's planting of informal areas, which were sometimes arranged around exotics (as an orchard of unusual Japanese cherries) or featured the display of certain flowers in a wooded setting (as the Japanese tree peony). Her informal gardens might abut enclosed gardens, their plantings, especially the trees (fig. 50), working together to form a complete composition.

In contrast to both her formal and informal gardens is the naturalistic garden, where meadow and woodland prevail but where carefully inserted planting improves upon natural conditions. It is opposite in concept to the enclosed garden as it does not have defineable boundaries but merges into the surrounding wild or semi-wild landscape (fig. 51). This quality of blending is of great importance; although a great many plants are introduced, the effect is intended to be as if the plants had always been there, having only been discovered (see pl. XV).

Although Farrand incorporated this naturalistic use of plants in many of her designs, most notably on her college campuses and in her more complex gardens, such as Dumbarton Oaks or Reef Point, her naturalistic plantings are difficult to find today because most have reverted to the wild. The trees have closed in, and meadow and flowers have disappeared.

When the enclosed and informal gardens at Dumbarton Oaks were given by the Blisses to Harvard University in 1941, the extensive naturalistic portion, comprising twenty-six acres, was omitted. It was given instead to the National Park Service (to form a park adjacent to the Harvard-owned property) but was not long maintained by them and thus began to decline.

The development of a naturalistic landscape allows the designer the luxury of beginning a composition with many important elements already

51. View to the pastoral landscape beyond Dumbarton Oaks, 1938. Courtesy of Dumbarton Oaks, Trustees for Harvard University.

in place. The challenge is twofold: first to remove those parts of the composition which are invasive and which interfere with the scale of the whole, and then to add new plantings which will reinforce those already in place. By these means the landscape is changed from one that is wild to one that is naturalistic.

A landscape allowed to grow without maintenance proceeds to its inevitable forest conclusion. Unwanted plantings dominate, grasses invade, ponds fill in, a bog is created, then a moist woodland appears, and soon a leafy canopy covers all. The designer of a naturalistic garden must control this direction by active interference in the process to create an ideal, bucolic landscape. The ratio of open grassland to wood is important. The dark wood should have vistas to allow the visitor to look out onto grasslands, to lightness, warmth, and most importantly, safety. The feeling of well-being that is felt within such a pastoral landscape undoubtedly is the result of thousands of years of human experience, and it is only relatively recently that aesthetic theory has sought to explain it.

The landscape designer, in creating a naturalistic landscape, seeks to instill in the viewer that mystical feeling of well-being that occurs where nature has been improved upon in some subtle way. Thus the naturalistic garden requires as much design effort as do formal or informal gardens. More importantly, it requires as much maintenance to allow it to continue as a designed composition; otherwise it reverts to the wild and again becomes a closed rather than an open landscape, a wilderness rather than a pastoral scene.

Over the fireplace in the Music Room at Dumbarton Oaks is a topographical view of the gardens in 1935. This view is an excellent reminder of what the naturalistic part of the gardens once looked like. That part of the gardens has been allowed to grow with minimum maintenance since the 1950s. At present there is archaeological evidence of its former character—ponds and water courses which have silted up considerably—but the planting has changed dramatically. An invasion of trees has cut out the light and changed the landscape from meadow to forest. The topographic painting reveals broad sunny meadows and a wide trail with bridges which cross a stream at various places. Along the path are plantings in mass (fig. 52) that Jekyll would have approved for their "simplicity of aim." The stream, which

52. View in the naturalistic garden, Dumbarton Oaks, 1938. Courtesy of Dumbarton Oaks, Trustees for Harvard University.

had existed prior to the design of the Dumbarton Oaks Gardens, was changed considerably by Farrand to form a series of pools with waterfalls and bridges which echoed the stone structure of the more formal gardens in this most natural place.

Recently, a series of old silver-nitrate negatives of the gardens was discovered at Dumbarton Oaks. A portion of these photographs had been taken as a progressive series of record shots of Farrand's naturalistic garden. Thanks to this discovery, we are able to see today exactly what she intended and how portions of this garden looked in her time. The photographs appear to have been taken after 1935 but before 1939. Although there are other photographs of her naturalistic plantings, this series is of exceptional value.

53. The Forsythia Dell entry to the naturalistic garden, Dumbarton Oaks, 1935; detail of a watercolor by Ernest Clegg. Courtesy of Dumbarton Oaks, Trustees for Harvard University.

It reveals the nature of Beatrix Farrand's planting in detail. Because the photographs were taken in early spring, aspects of landscape construction are also clearly visible and subtleties which would be covered by summer foliage are revealed. In addition, we are able to see the clarity of the connection between the informal and naturalistic parts of the garden, a connection almost impossible to read in the landscape as it exists today.

A major approach to the naturalistic garden, specifically to a rustic shelter at the edge of a stream, was through the Forsythia Dell (fig. 53). A well-constructed combination of stone stairs and ramps descends the steep hillside (fig. 54), with high mounds of forsythia cascading on either side. The pale yellow of the forsythia in spring would set the mood for the delicate yellows, light greens, purples, and blues to be found below. When the forsythia was not in bloom, the fresh green monochromatic foliage color prepared one for the greater complexity of light and shadow in the woodland garden. At the edge of the forsythia planting were silver maples, con-

54. The entrance to the naturalistic garden through the Forsythia Dell, Dumbarton Oaks, 1938, with *Acer saccharinum* in the background. Courtesy of Dumbarton Oaks, Trustees for Harvard University.

sidered by Farrand to be the most graceful American hardwood, far surpassing any other tree. The effect of this long descent, literally enveloped by cascading forsythia, is one which can no longer be experienced because the property dividing-line now cuts across the lower section of the stairway and the forsythia itself is now maintained in a much tidier manner than Farrand intended, not being allowed to touch the sides of the walk itself.

Another path led to the woodland through an informal part of the gardens where one could walk more freely and on a slope less severe. This gravel path led through low azaleas and crowded daffodils.

Prior to planting the naturalistic garden, Farrand evaluated this portion of the existing landscape and recommended a considerable number of tree removals. A portion of the property had been farmed prior to its development by the Blisses, therefore a large part was already meadowland and required only refinement in the removal of trees in order to allow more light to penetrate and at the same time to provide space for naturalistic plantings, such as a hillside of *Kalmia latifolia* (fig. 55) and another of gray birch where the Jekyll conception of "breadth" could again be achieved.

The serpentine line beloved of the romantics (fig. 56) appears as an important part of the Dumbarton Oaks naturalistic garden, and, as laid out by Farrand, is always successful in arousing curiosity, inviting further exploration to be rewarded with a new, but never final, discovery. (This sequential development in the natural garden is experienced in her formal gardens as well. The whole is not perceived at once, and movement is encouraged.) In this instance, one side of the path is formally retained with rounded stones from the stream bed, while the other, near the bank, is more casually arranged with stones at irregular intervals. The plantings along the path and in the meadow reveal a mixture of thinning and new planting to create an effect of naturalism.

As the path progresses into denser woods, a number of clearings allow the introduction of flowering plants, including *Althaea rosea*—its clear white blossoms with deep red centers set off to great advantage against the dark shade. These introduced plantings along the stream bed give added texture and, more importantly, bloom during the summer and fall. Most of the introduced plantings are, however, woodland types, with emphasis placed on laurel, rhododendron, and fern. Ferns soften the stonework of a rustic arbor,

55. A hillside of *Kalmia latifolia* in the naturalistic garden, Dumbarton Oaks, 1938. Courtesy of Dumbarton Oaks, Trustees for Harvard University.

the seat of which has been cut into the hillside (fig. 57). The lines of the seat and of the arbor itself are gently curving and the arbor is constructed with great simplicity—it is the most rustic arbor at Dumbarton Oaks (fig. 58 offers a comparison)—yet the proportions are as elegant as the most exquisite detail of the grand staircase in the formal gardens.

The rustic arbor overlooks a pond, created by damming the stream, and out to a gently rising hillside which has been planted with drifts of daffodils and a small copse of newly-planted *Cornus florida alba* (fig. 59). This lost landscape was at the same time intimate and expansive, providing the pastoral outlook required to make the naturalistic garden a success. Mildred Bliss kept her horses here, and the paths in this part of the grounds led to the riding trails in adjacent Rock Creek Park. A great sense of spaciousness

56. The serpentine path along the stream bed in the naturalistic garden, Dumbarton Oaks, 1938. Courtesy of Dumbarton Oaks, Trustees for Harvard University.

was given to the gardens at Dumbarton Oaks because of their relation to this park, but also because the meadowlands on the property were kept open, not overgrown as they are today.

The water courses in Farrand's design were artfully done; they significantly changed the landscape from wild to naturalistic because of the variety of their treatment and because they obviously signified the designer's intervention. It was by means of this watercourse and these naturalistic meadowlands that Mildred Bliss was able to realize most clearly her dream of being in the countryside while at the same time living in Washington, D.C.

GARDEN DESIGN THROUGH TIME

Beatrix Farrand, more than most landscape architects, believed very strongly in the necessity for continuity of supervision and for active intervention by the designer in the development of a garden over an extended period of time. She believed, and attempted to convince her clients, that the achievement of a garden as a work of art was something that could be accomplished only by constant refinement. This approach, which she considered to be a part of the design process, took into consideration the dynamic quality of garden design, the fact that plants are living organisms, that each plant goes through its cycle of seed, vegetative growth, and reproduction in its unique way. All gardens are composed of complex groups of individual plants. Through the designer's plans and repeated interventions, the interrelationships are controlled and arranged to produce a particular effect. This approach to planting design goes beyond the designer's supervision of maintenance. It calls for a much more active involvement throughout the life of the garden. It can be expressed in the following principle: continuity in design plus careful supervision of maintenance are fundamental to a beautiful garden. This formula takes into consideration the dynamics of change inherent in the plants used and emphasizes the role of time in landscape design. The works which were most satisfying to Beatrix Farrand as a designer were those in which this long-term design process was possible. At Dumbarton Oaks, her most gratifying project, she worked intensively for twenty years (1921–1941) and continued as a consultant to Harvard University for another six. She worked at the Rockefeller garden in Seal Harbor, Maine for twenty-four years

57. The rustic arbor in the naturalistic garden, Dumbarton Oaks, 1938. Courtesy of Dumbarton Oaks, Trustees for Harvard University.

58. *Wisteria sinensis* on an arbor just outside the northeast corner of the Rose Garden, Dumbarton Oaks, 1978. Courtesy of Dumbarton Oaks, Trustees for Harvard University.

(1926–1950) and at the Milliken garden in Northeast Harbor for twenty (1925–1945). The same extended effort characterized her major campus commissions: thirty-one years at Princeton University (1912–1943), twenty-three at Yale (1922–1945).

This extended activity enabled Farrand to refine and regulate the annual changes in the garden, as well as to oversee the removal, replacement, and additions required for its more permanent structure. In many instances she kept a separate garden account for a job, which would be paid into in advance by the client. She would make up the orders for seeds and bulbs which would then be sent upon receipt to the gardener at the site. This assured her that the the color schemes which she had carefully worked out would remain intact, and it also gave her the opportunity to change, experiment, and, most importantly, to retain control.

Farrand's involvement often went beyond matters of design and execution. An interesting example of her attention to detail can be found in a letter she addressed to Anne Sweeney, who was developing an educational lecture on the gardens subsequent to their transfer to Harvard University, and who had submitted the manuscript to Farrand for approval.[11] Farrand's attention to this lecture is representative of the care she gave to every aspect of her projects, not just her plantings.

Dear Miss Sweeney:

Don't condemn me for having delayed so long in returning the manuscript of your preliminary talk. I have wanted to go over it with considerable care for many reasons: first, because you and I are engaged in a very important sort of enterprise which we want to make a real success; second, because Mrs. Bliss will undoubtedly hear repercussions of your guide service and we want them to be entirely favorable and, as you and I both know, she has a mercifully wise and critical mind. I am therefore returning you your manuscript very much rewritten and altered and don't know whether the changes will be possible to decipher or not. If I had more time . . . I would have rewritten the whole script for you.

You must be very sure of the correctness of your statements. In the first place, you are wrong in saying Acer saccharinum is an imported tree. It is an American and therefore can't be called "introduced." . . .

Also be very sure you have the references correct as to the origins of your plants. Rosa rugosa, for instance, comes from North China, Korea or Japan. Pyracantha is a "cousin" of the thorns (Rosaceae) but not a barberry at all. The Kentucky Coffee Tree is its name, not the Kentucky Coffee Berry Tree.

The fastigiate shape of the tree is named from fasti, a peaked gable, and the flame shape is merely the shape of the candle flame, but not the origin of the name of it.

To go on still further, on page 4 are you sure that the Forsythia is suspensa? My impression is that it is one of the intermedia × spectabilis types.

59. Hillside opposite the rustic arbor in the naturalistic garden, Dumbarton Oaks, 1938. Courtesy of Dumbarton Oaks, Trustees for Harvard University.

On page 7 you had better verify as to the Beardless Iris coming to us from China. My impression is that many of the parents are European, such as Florentina, Plicata, and so on.

In fact, go over the script with a tooth comb and catch any further like inaccuracies which have escaped my eye. It won't do to have us telling people that the silver maple comes to us from China when the learned know that it is an American tree, to be found in many a moist woodlot.

It would be also wise policy to mention our Prairie Rose (Rosa setigera) as it is the parent of some of the most promising new hybrids. . . .

On page 8, it might be well to digress and say that the Yews are a very interesting family, allied to the conifers, very ancient in their origin and having this peculiar fleshy envelope to their little seed.

You might mention the fact also that Taxaceae are found in fossils together with the ginkgo and the great mosslike trees which survive today in the little club mosses.

It might be well, on page 9, to mention the fact that the apple spoken of in the Garden of Eden is in all likelihood some semi-tropical desert fruit and was called "apple" by the translators who did not know the English equivalent for the Hebrew plant, just as the Lily of the Field is thought to have been the Anemone of Palestine rather than our garden lilies.

You will find that your talk is a little too brief so that a little padding of this sort will be useful and can be fitted in on separate leaves which can be used for different groups at various seasons. It might be wise for you to keep a series of these separate slips with comments on the different seasons as you observe them. For instance, this talk of yours will not be of very much use in the winter, when you will need to speak of winter buds, branching, and the characteristic shape of the trees. . . .

I have not looked up the Chinese quince tree but you had better be sure that this is the correct name. I know that the quince has gone through two or three alterations in the last fifteen or twenty years.

On page 12, add more as to the Buttercup family, speaking of the other garden favorites which are members of the family, like anemone, delphinium, meadow rue, aconite, globe flower, etc. It might be well also somewhere in the talk to add a little aside, mentioning how many of the garden flowers we owe to our own country, and speak of phlox, coreopsis, rudbeckia, most of the lupins, and the others from Mexico like ageratum, dahlia, salvia. Another aside would allow you to tell your hearers that it is thought that the great reservoir of the Rhododendron species probably lies northeast of the Himalayas between China, Tibet and India, as many hundred sorts have been found in this particular neighborhood, both growing in the tropical forest and dwarfed to the size of creeping phlox on the mountain tops. All of these odds and ends interest people, even though they may not apply to Dumbarton Oaks itself.

You might also make a further aside on the contribution of the rose family with its fruits—cherry, pear, apple, plum, quince, strawberry, blackberry—and its flowers—spiraea, cotoneaster, thorns, mountain ash.

Then it might be worthwhile to make a sort of little gallery of portraits of the different trees so that you can vary your talks. Give your description of Acer saccharinum and mention the fact that its name is easily confused with that of Acer saccharum, and here you can say how confusing some of the nomenclature is, as names were bandied about in the early days, sometimes from one plant to another. For instance you might mention the Douglas spruce, and its various names and transformations. See in Rehder the list of synonyms. Its name now, as you know, is pseudo tsuga taxifolia, but look, in the description following its name, at the different names it has appeared under!—at least five and I think a good many more. Then you might also very wisely tell people why the Latin names of plants are essential to accuracy and mention this same Douglas spruce. In the northwest it is called fir, sometimes red, sometimes white. In England it is called Douglas fir. In the old days, it used to be called hemlock. In the east, it is usually known as the Douglas spruce.

You speak, on page 14, of the Bamboos and say they are native to Japan. They are native, not only to Japan, but to a very large realm of the southeast Asiatic tropics and they are the staff of life without which many of these races simply could not live. They make containers, mattings, thatches, houses, cooking utensils, implements, boats, hunting implements, whereas here in this part of the world we meet it mainly in the shape of porch furniture.

On page 14, one of your best paragraphs is the one about the ginkgo.

Another portrait study would be one of the American elm, its association with New England, its incomparable fountain form, and mention the present diseases which now endanger its life. Mention its approximate length of life, which is not supposed to run over a hundred and fifty or two hundred years, in comparison with the oak lifespan which will run perhaps to six or seven hundred. . . .

Again, on page 15, be very sure you make it clear that the Buttonwood (Platanus occidentalis) is not the same tree as Platanus orientalis, the tree of which Egyptian mummy cases were made.

In speaking of Magnolia denudata, I don't think you are correct in saying that conspicua is a variety. I think it is a synonym (a former name).

Also, it might be worthwhile to mention the peculiarity of so many Chinese plants, which show their flowers before the leaves, Magnolia denudata, Forsythia, some of the plums and I think some of the pears. There must be some physiological reason for this flowering before the leaving, but it is worth mentioning as a characteristic of plants in certain Asiatic regions.

60. *Buxus sempervirens, Pieris japonica,* and katsura at Dumbarton Oaks, 1979. Photograph: Ursula Pariser.

When you speak of the white oak, you are confining it to the northeastern United States, whereas I think the tree runs pretty well into the south central states also. Rehder gives it as running from New England to Florida, west to Minnesota and Texas, so that the northeastern United States is only one of its habitats. The same remark about "introduced about 1724" can hardly be applied. Although Rehder gives this, it would mean that it was then introduced to cultivation. Evidently my remark is wrong about "introduce" not being applicable to a native as Rehder bears you out, and he is the final authority.

Don't think I have gone over your talk with an unkindly comb. I have tried to add any such scraps here and there as might be useful and give variety, and the criticisms I have made are the ones that you would wish me to make in the interests of accuracy for the University as well as for yourself.

61. Box Border leading south at the corner of the east lawn, Dumbarton Oaks, 1979. Photograph: Ursula Pariser.

PLANTS COMMONLY USED BY BEATRIX FARRAND

A great many of the plants used by Beatrix Farrand are still popular today. She used plants which were in the mainstream of cultivation in her time, preferring the tried and true varieties. *Buxus sempervirens* (figs. 60 & 61) and *Buxus sempervirens* 'Suffruticosa' are still offered, and they are used in quantity by gardeners because, as Beatrix Farrand asserted, no other plant provides the texture and delicacy of scale throughout the year and offers such a strong background as does the boxwood.

Similarly *Berberis verruculosa* and *Forsythia intermedia* 'Spectabilis' continue to be favored by the gardening public, although in the matter of the forsythias several new varieties have been introduced. Beatrix Farrand favored *F. intermedia* 'Spectabilis' because of its good color, large size, and the fact that it is the most floriferous of all the forsythias (described by Isabel Zucker as "a living bouquet"[12]). When its effect is multiplied over one acre of land, as it is in the Forsythia Dell at Dumbarton Oaks, the value of massing one color over a large area is readily seen. This plant, which seldom has a problem of insects or disease and which spreads its branches in a delicate, graceful arch, also formed the backbone of many of Farrand's northeastern campus plantings and was a strong second in the parade of spring-flowering shrubs, following the witch hazel.

In her California work, Farrand used plants which we associate with Mediterranean plantings. They were the plants which she had seen on her travels abroad—the laurel, myrtle, pomegranate, and olive in Italy, for example. These were all plants that had strong historical or literary associations which related them more closely to Europe than California. Her designs were carried out with plantings which grew well in the California climate but were expressive of a different culture and another period.

Ground Covers and Wall Plants

Farrand relied heavily on ground covers, especially *Hedera helix* 'Baltica' (fig. 62) and *Vinca minor,* to achieve important design effects in the garden and in the broader landscape. Baltic Ivy was introduced by the Arnold Arboretum from the Baltic provinces of Russia, and it proved hardier than any other form. Since ivy both clings and trails along the ground, it was the most free-ranging plant that she used. At times it was allowed to grow rampantly on a hillside, while not obscuring the curve of the land. Then again, it could, through clipping, be strictly contained on a fence or a wall (fig. 63), or trained to curve in and out of a balustrade, allowing the architectural form to show but at the same time softening it considerably. When climate allowed, she added *Jasminum nudiflorum* (fig. 64), the bright yellow flowers cascading against the background of the Baltic ivy, thereby opposing the play of brilliants to the dark green, partial covering of the architecture. The line between ground cover and vine was continually crossed and recrossed.

62. *Hedera helix* 'Baltica' used as a ground cover and wall planting with *Pieris japonica* at the entry to the copse, Dumbarton Oaks, 1980. Courtesy of Dumbarton Oaks, Trustees for Harvard University.

63. *Hedera helix* 'Baltica' as a wall planting at Dumbarton Oaks. Courtesy of Dumbarton Oaks, Trustees for Harvard University.

Another reason Baltic ivy was of artistic importance to Farrand as a ground cover was because it turned partially bronze in winter. The green changed to a black-green which heightened contrast when it was used, as it frequently was, in conjunction with architectural stonework and sculpture.

A different opportunity existed in her use of *Vinca minor*. Examining old photographs of Farrand gardens reveals that in certain areas the idea of creeping, twining ground covers was very much favored, and in the same gardens, architectural control of plants through clipping and severe pruning was also carried out. These two approaches contrasted and added to the richness of the display. Vinca with its long, twining stems was luxuriant as it cascaded down hillsides, its beautiful blue flowers adding to the cheerfulness of late spring. Indeed the vinca was often a covering for the spent foliage of drifts of narcissus and grape hyacinths. Also it provided, as, for example, on the Green Terrace at Dumbarton Oaks, a softer alternative to the tidiness of a mown lawn.

It is generally true today that we do not exploit the use of vines to the degree that was fashionable before the 1930s. Yet a larger number of vines is available in the nursery trade today. In addition to the *Clematis paniculata* and *C.* 'Duchess of Edinburgh', *Lonicera japonica halliana,* and *Wisteria sinensis* which continue to be favorites, we find today many new introductions of clematis and wisteria.

An examination of photographs of gardens built in the first twenty-five years of this century reveals unmistakeably the interest of many landscape designers in shrouding garden walls, garden buildings, pergolas, well-heads, and balustrades with heavy curtains of foliage, sometimes in layers so dense that one must merely make the assumption that they conceal a structure of some sort. This heaviness of planting frequently resulted in a wild tangle, appearing as if the garden had been abandoned for a number of years. This deliberate, heavy-curtained appearance had its origins in late-nineteenth-century studies of Italian villas, many of which were in a state of romantic disrepair. Their vines, particularly, not being maintained, had grown in an uncontrolled manner. Added to this influence was the example of the exuberance of the roses grown in the English cottage garden, where a lack of control was also considered to be "romantic." In American gardens these models were often misinterpreted, in the form of roses completely covering

64. *Jasminum nudiflorum, Hedera helix* 'Baltica' and stone sculpture at Dumbarton Oaks. Courtesy of Dumbarton Oaks, Trustees for Harvard University.

arbors or pillars hidden under ivy to the extent that brick or stone was completely invisible. Wisteria clothed surfaces, disguising, and in many cases, disfiguring architecture, so that a porch appeared as a series of lumps, without a visible roof and without a sense of support. The garden visitor was awash in a restless green sea. Such gardens lacked structure. The hard lines of architecture were not just softened but were frequently erased.

Beatrix Farrand used vines and many types of wall plants in her work, but she did it with a difference (fig. 65). Two of her strongest assets as a designer were her sense of proportion and her understanding of structure and the materials from which structures are made. Her unerring sense of fitness, of a correct relationship between garden structure and overall layout

65. Roses and wisteria trained on the south front of the orangery at Dumbarton Oaks, with *Buxus sempervirens* in the foreground. Courtesy of Dumbarton Oaks, Trustees for Harvard University.

66. Wall plantings and *Ulmus americana* at the superintendant's cottage, Dumbarton Oaks. Courtesy of Dumbarton Oaks, Trustees for Harvard University.

and the buildings contained therein, appeared in her earliest work and formed a consistent pattern as her work progressed (figs. 66 & 67). It explains the success of many of her designs.

She established a clear relationship between wall plants and the architecture they enhanced (fig. 68). In some instances, the structure of a vine carried out an architectural motif, similar to that of a bas-relief. The remaining wisteria at Yale has this sculptural quality because it has been clipped and trimmed through the years with the idea of containing it and modeling it to fit the architecture. It has not been allowed to become wild and free-ranging, but works with the architecture rather than obscuring the facade and its prominent details. In many instances the choice of vine color had the additional advantage of complementing the color of the wall on which it

67. The entrance balustrade and *Hedera helix* 'Baltica' at Dumbarton Oaks, 1938. Courtesy of Dumbarton Oaks, Trustees for Harvard University.

well. Because the viewing machine was intended to increase the appearance of perspective, the views were originally drawn and then engraved to emphasize the dominance of the central perspective. Many gardens, in their relation to villas or palaces, were delineated in this manner.) Central to her interest was the mass and detail of the buildings and the relationship of gardens to them. She studied her engravings carefully and eventually made them a part of the study collection she established at Reef Point.

Her interest in architecture was manifested by her controlled use of wall plantings and also by the relationships she established between different structural elements in her gardens and the visual sightlines which resulted from her location of these structural elements. In a great many of her projects she worked directly with the architect, and sometimes undertook a considerable amount of architectural work herself. As is often the case in the practice of landscape architecture, the degree of influence one has regarding the final appearance of the project depends to a great extent on the willingness of the architect to collaborate. Farrand's most successful projects were those in which her involvement in the architectural design was most extensive, where she worked directly with the architect in the establishment of the key points of relationship between structure and planting.

There were instances where Farrand's use of wall plants and trellis work gave interest to facades that needed to be concealed rather than emphasized (figs. 70 & 71). In explanation of her treatment of the walls facing the Dumbarton Oaks Green Terrace, she wrote:

> *On the east wall of the drawing room are espaliered* Magnolia grandiflora, *which have to be controlled with considerable skill so that they do not become too insistent and enveloping. Some heavy planting, however, is useful in masking the awkward angle between the corner of the connecting passageway to the flower room and roof balcony and the east wall of the drawing room. This is a small re-entering angle, which, if not filled with foliage, makes an unfortunate line.*[13]

Even at her most flamboyant, Farrand exercised restraint. She demanded a high and exacting level of maintenance, which allowed her wall plantings to become more impressive as the years went on. Although she

70. *Ampelopsis heterophylla,* jasmine, and wisteria near an arbor built against a retaining wall, Dumbarton Oaks, 1938. Courtesy of Dumbarton Oaks, Trustees for Harvard University.

71. Trellis and stone bench at Dumbarton Oaks. Courtesy of Dumbarton Oaks, Trustees for Harvard University.

was influenced in her use of vines by Jekyll, Farrand was much less inclined to have vines become truly a tangle; her sense of propriety and architectural integrity dominated. Her European travel very likely provided her with the initial models for this type of work, as it has never been characteristic of American landscape architecture.

In addition to the obvious vines such as wisteria, ivy, and roses, which grew easily in the wall position and could be carefully controlled, there were other plants that Farrand established on walls which gave distinction to the architecture. Probably the most important in this category was the previously mentioned *Magnolia grandiflora* (fig. 72), which she had seen abroad used as a wall plant, but which in America was almost always grown as a large, specimen, broad-leaf evergreen tree placed so as to make it a central feature or to mark the terminus of a design. Directly influenced by Gertrude Jekyll, Farrand saw the value of this tree in offering a contrast to the usual wall plant because of its extraordinarily large scale, strong green color, and noble, polished foliage. Its large leaves provided excellent contrast with the evergreen ivy with which she often combined it, but it was necessary to keep the foliage as flat to the wall as possible to achieve the desired effect, which meant constant vigilance in pruning.

In her campus designs, wall plants were of considerable importance. They were one of the three planting elements—trees, lawn (sward), and vines—by means of which she was able to achieve the desired combination of beauty and utility in the design of courtyards. Shrubs played a secondary role in her courtyard designs. She used them instead (especially the native types) in large masses where larger-scale plantings were needed in the open landscape. By keeping her courtyards largely free of shrubs and relying instead on wall plantings, she made them appear large, simple, and dignified, the lawns providing an apron for the display of the architecture.

Deciduous Shrubs

Shrubs were important in Beatrix Farrand's gardens. *Abelia grandiflora* was a versatile plant in her palette. She used it primarily because it combined exceptionally well with broadleaf and needle evergreens and this combination retained its effect into late fall and early winter (depending on climate) because of the bronzy color of the abelia in autumn and its deep bronze-purple in winter. It is an exceptionally beautiful shrub, of great elegance in habit, with small, glossy leaves. In late June it has pale pink, tubular flowers in star-like clusters. After the flowers go by, the rose-colored calyx dominates and is more effective than the flowers themselves. Farrand frequently used glossy abelia with *Hedera helix* 'Baltica' as a ground cover beneath and as a climbing vine on a wall behind.

Berberis thunbergi was used by Farrand primarily in her campus plantings, but it appears with some regularity in her other work as well. She used it as a specimen plant; in plantings near buildings and interwoven in shrub borders; and also frequently as a hedge. She used it for campus planting because of its scarlet autumn leaf-color and persistent red berries. Moreover, Japanese barberry is a most undemanding plant, not particular as to soil type. It will grow in semishade and in full sun and will tolerate dryness better than most deciduous shrubs. Therefore, it requires little maintenance. However, where it has persisted in her campus plantings it has frequently

72. *Magnolia grandiflora* grown as a wall planting at the 32nd Street entrance, Dumbarton Oaks, 1978. Photograph: Ursula Pariser.

taken on a ragged appearance due to improper pruning. When it is shaped into dreadful little balls, the graceful arching of the branches, which particularly appealed to Farrand, is lost completely.

Cydonia japonica, known today as *Chaenomeles speciosa* (the flowering quince) has changed its name several times, but Farrand knew it as *Cydonia* and it is still listed as such in some nursery catalogs, where it remains a popular item. Two beautiful single white varieties, 'Candida' and 'Nivalis', were introduced to this country in the latter half of the nineteenth century. Farrand used them extensively in her campus landscape plantings for several reasons. They have the great advantage of flowering in the early spring, with a flower of the greatest delicacy. The plant is very hardy, undemanding as to soil requirements, and requires the most minimal pruning in order to look well.

The deutzias as a group are outstanding low-maintenance plants, but only the slender deutzia (*Deutzia gracilis*) also bears beautiful, delicate clear-white flowers in late May, doing this so profusely that it can dominate visually, during its blooming period, an area much greater than its small size would suggest. That size made it difficult for Farrand to combine it readily with other plants, which tended to overwhelm it, but she valued it for its display. She used it very successfully in pairs as marker plants, where attention could be attracted without taking away from the general uniformity of a background planting. She was concerned that too many "incidents of planting" would make her designs too busy, counteracting her preferred restful effect. *Deutzia gracilis* is a plant that was grown very early at the Arnold Arboretum, and Farrand would have been able to study it there.

Forsythia intermedia 'Spectabilis' is the variety Farrand chose to plant in the famous Forsythia Dell (pl. VI) at Dumbarton Oaks (fig. 73). Its intense cascade of yellow in early April is, along with the cherry blossoms on the Potomac, one of the great sights of a Washington spring. Unfortunately, at Dumbarton Oaks, both the brilliant yellow of the forsythia and the more delicate pink of a cherry orchard next to it appear at exactly the same time, and they do not harmonize well because the intensity of the forsythia is overpowering.

Forsythia is found in a great many of Farrand's campus plantings as well as in her private gardens. It is a shrub of substantial scale. She often used several varieties in order to prolong the period of bloom. She favored forsythia for its graceful arching branches, a virtue she felt to be foremost in considering the habit of deciduous shrubs. Quantities of forsythia were also planted at Dumbarton Oaks for forcing.

Hybiscus syriacus is an especially useful shrub for the landscape designer because it blooms at a time—late summer—when few other woody plants are in bloom. It also has a narrow upright form which makes it easy to plant in combination with other deciduous material. The single white is the variety of shrub althea usually specified by Farrand.

Hydrangea arborescens 'Grandiflora', a showy native plant, is widely admired for its creamy white blossoms in early July, but it is also easy to transplant and to grow. Farrand used it in masses, where the effect was impressive and elegant. The luminous green of its foliage makes it an excellent background for other plantings even when it is not in bloom. This plant was used by Farrand in informal gardens because of its semiwild qualities; it

73. *Forsythia intermedia* 'Spectabilis' at Dumbarton Oaks, 1978. Courtesy of Dumbarton Oaks, Trustees for Harvard University.

grows very well at the edge of woods where its refined appearance has a civilizing effect.

Ligustrum vulgaris, the common privet, was used by Farrand in a number of ways. Privets made excellent low-cost hedges, but she also planted them in quantity in more informal arrangements, allowing them to develop their handsome natural form and their fragrant flowers. The versatility of the privet, as well as its modest maintenance requirements and ease of propagation, made it a superior candidate for institutional planting, and it frequently appears in her campus plant lists. It also combines well with deciduous plants, and she used it often in a mixed border for a deciduous screen effect.

Lonicera fragrantissima (fragrant honeysuckle) is an upright-growing plant with long stiff branches that spread outward and arch. Its leaves are thick and dark green, although without fall color. Its large size and dark foliage give it a place of distinction in the shrub border. Farrand used it for its landscape value, as it becomes a handsome cascading plant with proper pruning; but she used it also for its intense fragrance. It is one of the earliest shrubs to bloom in spring and among the longest lasting.

The mock oranges (*Philadelphus coronarius*) as a group are especially suited for large-scale plantings. They are not particular about soil and do not require much attention once established. Mock orange is relatively insect-free and highly tolerant of dryness. Its flowers are extremely fragrant, a blend of orange fruit and jasmine. Generally, only a small amount of renewal pruning is needed every few years. Yet, because it is often planted in too small a space, *Philadelphus coronarius,* which normally achieves ten feet in height and six in width, is often pruned in a devastating way, becoming a mass of uninteresting twigs. Farrand used mock orange for screening and for background effects. She also used it extensively near college buildings, where its large scale is appropriate with the building size. Its early June blooming period made it appropriate at colleges at commencement.

Ribes odoratum, a native plant of the midwest, was a popular, old-fashioned favorite. It is seen less frequently in gardens today because it is a host for white-pine blister-rust. Farrand used it for its intense fragrance. Helen van Pelt Wilson has described it as "showy as forsythia but with the scent of a thousand pinks."[14] Not reaching above six feet, it suckers and grows in beautiful little clumps, suiting it well to an informal garden. *Ribes odoratum* is a plant frequently found in abandoned gardens. Perhaps because it is a native, or possibly because of its habit of suckering, it persists even when neglected, providing a gorgeous spring display of yellow color and then, in autumn, turning a brilliant scarlet.

Farrand also used a great many roses in her landscape schemes, choosing them primarily for their color, in formal rose gardens, and for their fragrance in less formal parts of the garden. As mentioned earlier, she frequently used climbers to grow on pergolas, trellises, and garden fences. In studying what remains of Farrand's gardens in the field, it is always a pleasure to find that the old climbers have persisted, often outlasting the pergolas and trelisses they grew upon.

Farrand's taste in roses was far simpler than that of her clients, who frequently asked for ostentatious hybrids in complicated plantings. Her preference was for the simpler forms of roses. In her own rose garden at Reef Point she clustered her roses near the house on the east-facing terrace where their elegant beauty and fragrance were close at hand.

Spiraea prunifolia, an old-fashioned plant with rather delicate scale, was often used by Farrand because of its showy qualities. The bridal-wreath spirea has a white, button-like bloom in mid-May, effective for several weeks. It also has excellent, glossy green foliage in spring and summer, which in autumn turns to a lustrous orange. In the fall, *Spiraea prunifolia* is especially effective in rain, as its delicate branches become very black, thereby heightening contrast in the garden. Farrand often relied on this spirea when she needed a plant of refined scale in her campus plantings. *Spiraea prunifolia* combines well with other deciduous plants and also looks well by itself in a large grouping, which was the way she frequently used it.

Farrand used many hybrids of the common purple lilac (*Syringa vulgaris*). Lilacs are considered by most to be a part of our native American landscape. Their association with American farms and building sites is taken for granted. Yet they were introduced from eastern Europe in early colonial times. Farrand let them grow boldly as screen plantations in informal settings. She also used them in more contrived ways, as at Dumbarton Oaks where she planted a circular hedge of lilacs surrounding a carpet of lily-of-the-valley bordered by day lilies—the Lilac Circle.

Trees

The large broad-leaved trees that build up the great hardwood forests of Europe and North America give us the grandest ornaments for landscape planting. The Norway maple (*Acer platanoides*), which was introduced from Europe and is also common in the gardens of southern England, was used primarily by Beatrix Farrand in her planting plans for northern colleges. Its rounded, dense form makes it especially useful for avenue planting, where dignity of structure is a primary requisite. The Norway maple provides interest at key times in the academic year. In late March, when little else is happening in deciduous trees, its bright, acid yellow-green flowers appear, before the leaves, soon carpeting the ground beneath the branches. In fall, the leaves of the Norway maple are a brilliant, butter-like yellow, contrasting dramatically with the darkness of the trunk. In deepest winter, the angle of the sun penetrates to advantage the deeply-fissured bark.

Acer saccharinum, previously known as *Acer dasycarpum* (the silver maple), is the only native American maple commonly planted in Britain, where it is used primarily for its graceful form and delicacy of appearance. Farrand recognized the distinctive qualities of the silver maple and she used it for artistic effect in several interesting ways. At Dumbarton Oaks, she found several trees growing on a hillside, cleared the hillside except for the maples, and made an underplanting of *Forsythia intermedia,* thereby creating the famous Forsythia Dell. The graceful swaying movement of the silver maple harmonizes with the billowing of forsythia. Also, at Dumbarton Oaks, the silver maple appears as a central specimen tree above the swimming pool, and two parallel rows of silver maples form an *allée* beyond the formal gardens at the eastern edge of the property. Farrand considered the silver maple among the most beautiful of trees because of its elegant form, free from the slightest degree of stiffness, and because of its sharply-cut leaves.

Gracefulness in appearance is the quality which Beatrix Farrand most admired in the deodar cedar (fig. 74). She considered *Cedrus deodara* to be the finest needle evergreen and she used it extensively for screen plantings or as a windbreak, and often used it in pairs to frame a distant view or object. The deodar cedar is characterized by a narrow, spire top with a drooping leading shoot. It also droops elegantly at the branch tips. These characteristics are enhanced when several trees are grown together to form a small grove. Although Farrand used other needle evergreens, especially spruce, she felt that the majority of needle evergreen trees were much too stiff to combine successfully with other types of plantings. The deodar cedar, because of its fluid grace, was an exception, and she used it many times, in a manner which seems natural.

Specimens of *Fagus grandiflora,* the European beech, now sixty or seventy years old and impressive in size and structure, are in several cases (as, for example, in courtyards at Yale and Princeton) the only survivors of Farrand's original plantings. Much else has vanished because of overcrowding or neglect. Yet the majestic beeches persist, dominating the spaces they oc-

74. *Cedrus deodara* with *Acer saccharinum,* weeping cherry, and weeping willow above the west wall of the swimming-pool terrace at Dumbarton Oaks, 1940. Courtesy of Dumbarton Oaks, Trustees for Harvard University.

cupy and providing visual interest, especially in spring when their delicate leaf-coloring appears and in winter when the silvery bark is most obvious. The European beech is widely planted in England, where it is used for the lining of avenues as well as in groves and as a specimen tree. Although relatively low in height, it is extensive in spread and a hardwood of extraordinarily dignified beauty. The copper beech, especially, provides the richest feast of color found in any tree, for sunlight penetrating to different depths of the canopy is reflected in varied shades, from russet to dark purple, which alter as the leaves are moved by the wind.

Ilex opaca, the American holly (fig. 75), is less showy than the English holly and generally thought to be less beautiful. Nevertheless, the American holly, with its sturdy appearance and lack of lustre in its leaves, was a favorite broadleaf evergreen in Beatrix Farrand's work and she used it in several ways, particularly in interesting combinations with other plants. She admired its color, the lighter green combining exceptionally well with boxwood and yew. This holly, yew, and box combination is used to great advantage at Dumbarton Oaks where, at the dramatic south entrance to the Rose Garden, a boxwood (inside the garden wall) and a yew (outside) surround a holly which, in its location outside the wall and directly next to the gate, is the key plant in a composition that signifies a transition from the formal garden to an informal woodland to the south.

The great English tree collections include *Liriodendron tulipifera* (tulip poplar) as representative of the finest of American hardwoods. Its straight

75. *Ilex opaca* and English box near the R Street entry, Dumbarton Oaks, 1938. Courtesy of Dumbarton Oaks, Trustees for Harvard University.

bole and great height (150 feet) make it particularly effective when planted near large buildings, as the scale is appropriate. The remarkable flower is hidden from the ground but may be viewed from second- and third-story windows. The little "candelabra" left on the tree all winter are also of decorative value. Farrand used the tulip poplar for many campus plantings and planted it in groves as a single species or mixed in plantations with other American hardwoods.

Magnolia denudata (yulan magnolia), a most beautiful tree, has fragrant flowers of an ivory color which bloom in early May. It also shows to advantage in fall, when its foliage becomes honey-brown in color, and in winter because of the nature of the twigs which are especially attractive with snow caught between the strong branchlets. In China, during the Jung Dynasty (A.D. 960–1260), *Magnolia denudata* was called "Ying-ch'un," meaning "meet the spring." There is an old specimen at Dumbarton Oaks in front of the orangery which Beatrix Farrand and Mildred Bliss referred to as "The Bride," because of its remarkable, ivory floral display each spring.

Magnolia grandiflora, the southern (or bull bay) magnolia, is the only evergreen magnolia with a glossy green leaf. It is a much admired tree, not only for its foliage but also because of its spectacular creamy-white flowers and curious fruit. It was introduced into England in 1734 where it is most commonly planted against walls. It is also frequently planted in that manner in Ireland. Once established against a wall it is a long-lived climber and its use on the walls of the British country house has made it a symbol of long-sustained affluence and gracious gardening. However, it is seldom grown in that manner in the United States, where it is much more frequently seen, in gardens of the South, as a free-standing tree. It is probable that in her travels in England, Beatrix Farrand saw *Magnolia grandiflora* grown against the walls of country houses. At Dumbarton Oaks, she established it against the house in several places, leaving instructions as to its periodic replacement and maintenance:

> *Plants of approximately ten to fifteen feet in height should be used for replacement, and should be chosen rather slender in their growth so that their branches may be trained and kept flattened to the wall, as is the custom with wall-trained Magnolia in Europe.*[15]

It is also grown at Dumbarton Oaks on several terrace walls combined with other climbers, as jasmine and Baltic ivy. More conventionally for America, it is used as a free-standing tree in front of the Fellows Building.

When Beatrix Farrand went to California in 1927, one of her earliest works there was at the Director's House at the Henry E. Huntington Library, where she constructed a garden for herself and her husband, Max Farrand, who had been appointed the first director. *Olea europaea* (common olive; pl. X) was used as the dominant feature of this garden and was also the backbone of the planting in the Humanities Garden that she designed at the California Institute of Technology. The olive, which she had seen many times in cultivation in southern Europe, seemed to her to have gracefulness, dignity and historical associations with the classical world that made it an appropriate tree to be used within an academic setting. Although other plantings have since died away in the Humanities Garden, and precious few are left at the Director's House, the *Olea europea* has persisted and is a dignified tree in its maturity, its graceful descending branches similar to those of the silver maple.

Beatrix Farrand valued many of the oaks, and she used them extensively in her campus plantings, where several varieties were often used to make a plantation. She chose the oaks for their sturdy growth, rich autumn color, height, and form. The oak, like holly, box, and yew, had strong associations with English landscape and garden plantings, being the commonest broadleaf tree in England. Moreover its landscape use at the turn of the century represented a return to traditional, homely plants, instead of the exotics characteristic of mid-nineteenth-century horticulture.

Charles Sprague Sargent, the first director of the Arnold Arboretum and Farrand's most influential teacher, knew the trees of North America as a horticulturist. He maintained that no conifer surpassed the hemlock in grace and beauty. Farrand used *Tsuga canadensis,* the Canadian hemlock, extensively in combination with broadleaf evergreens such as holly or *Pieris,* its texture forming a primary part of the composition. She also used it in her campus designs as screen planting or as an ornamental in courtyards where it could be shown to advantage against brick and stone. Hemlock is tolerant of dryness and general neglect; therefore it has persisted and survives in many of her campus plantings, although it is frequently overgrown.

76. *Ulmus americana* at the east end of the swimming pool at Dumbarton Oaks. Courtesy of Dumbarton Oaks, Trustees for Harvard University.

Associated closely with the earliest gardens in America, *Ulmus americana,* the American elm, like the silver maple, is still found today on historic properties and in the older parts of towns. This elm was introduced to England in 1752 but is rare there, found usually in collections. Farrand recognized the "incomparable beauty" of the American elm and she used it where its foliage and great arching limbs would be seen to greatest advantage, its spreading branches forming an important part of many of her compositions. This is well illustrated in figure 76, where the placement of two American elms at the end of the Dumbarton Oaks swimming pool lifts this part of the garden upward and provides a strong silhouette against the sky. The elm is characteristically a tree of descending branches, which gives it qualities of movement contributing greatly to the vitality of the composition.

77. Trees and grass in a courtyard at Princeton University, 1984. Photograph: Alan Ward.

CAMPUS WORK AND PUBLIC LANDSCAPES

DIANA BALMORI

Beatrix Farrand's campus work was much more important in the context of her total output than was previously thought or than the Farrand Document Collection at the University of California at Berkeley shows. It is in the lengthy correspondence with her University clients that a measure of it can be gained.[1] We see in the correspondence that her campus work extended over a long period of time (1912 to 1943 at Princeton, for example), that it grew in stature as it progressed, and that it forced Farrand to move from specific, individual designs to the formulation of general principles. In campus work, she created a philosophy of landscaping.

Moreover, in her campus work Farrand can be seen as a major representative of the Arts & Crafts Movement in United States landscape architecture. The principal exponents of the Arts & Crafts Movement, which got its start in England, were Augustus Pugin (1812–1852), John Ruskin (1819–1900), and William Morris (1834–1896). The movement sought simplicity in art, truth to materials, and the unity of craft and design. It turned to popular arts and crafts as the basis of inspiration for its design.

Private gardens were to Farrand a major source of enjoyment and delight. She called Dumbarton Oaks the "most deeply felt and best loved" work of a fifty-year practice. The campus work, in contrast, did not delight. Surviving in the public realm was always hard going. She faced the usual pejoratives applied to women who worked in a professional world from which they were customarily absent. The "bush-woman" they called her at Princeton and Yale.[2] But although she may not have found her campus work a constant source of personal pleasure, it was important as landscape. The nature of this campus landscaping is the subject of the pages that follow.

CAMPUS LANDSCAPING

Campus landscaping is not a major concern today. While older campuses still retain the atmosphere that good landscaping created, their appearance has deteriorated through the loss of plants and through ineffective standards of maintenance. In the 1890s, however, the situation was different: it was a time when the American campus changed dramatically in response to ideas from the Romantic movement; it was the time when American colleges and universities became campuses as we know them.

The term "campus" gained popular acceptance when the *Century Dictionary* of 1899 included the word in its lexicon. Princeton actually had coined the term in 1774 and used it to designate the university's grounds. In 1833, British author James Finch publicized the word in his *Travels in the United States and Canada:* "In front of the College [Princeton] is a fine campus with ornamented trees."

After the Civil War, other schools adopted the term.[3] At that time the physical appearance of American universities also changed: residential colleges were built in Gothic style and planned around a quadrangle—a response to the new ideal of a university as a small, self-contained community. Within these citadels of study, nature assumed a special role as restorer and stimulator. Derived from both the Romantic and the Arts & Crafts movements, this role assumed a new importance as American cities grew and became industrialized. The ideal university should now be set in nature (pl. XI).

Different colleges and universities sought nature in different ways. Some were established in rural settings far from large cities. Several, such as

Trinity at Hartford, moved out of the city. Even Yale attempted to leave New Haven for a more pastoral setting in the 1860s. Like others, however, it remained in the city but adopted the residential quadrangle and Gothic style, using their new courtyards to create green interior spaces. If a rural setting was impossible, the peaceful atmosphere of the countryside might thus be achieved within the city. This new ideal differed from the vision of the academic village at Thomas Jefferson's University of Virginia in that it sought, through the Gothic style and courtyard arrangement, ideals of a medieval past, and also in that it was a response to the appearance of the industrial city.

Into this movement stepped landscape gardener Beatrix Jones [Farrand]. In 1912, she was thirty years old and ready to begin her first job for a public institution—Princeton's new Graduate College. Yale, Oberlin, Chicago, Vassar, and Hamilton would also employ her services in the years to come. At Princeton and at Yale—two of the best examples of the new style of American campus—she would make her greatest impact.

Farrand came to Princeton specifically to design the landscape for the new Graduate College by architect Ralph Adams Cram. At Yale she began by landscaping the Harkness Memorial Quadrangle created by James Gamble Rogers. At each campus, these were the newest and most important examples of Collegiate-Gothic style, with buildings set as walls around inner courtyards. Each was the first residential complex on its campus.

The Arts & Crafts Movement, of which Cram was a prominent member, shaped this particularly important stage in the development of the American university campus. Beatrix Farrand undoubtedly had strong ties to the movement: the landscape principles and working methods that evolved in her campus activity clearly adhere to its philosophy and aesthetic.

Some general principles important to Farrand can be gathered from studying her work at the different campuses. These relate to the kinds of plants to be used (and where and how they were to be planted); to the shaping of the ground by contouring walks and steps; and to the creation of campus nurseries where experiments with plants could be carried out on the campus site.

Plants and Planting Methods

Farrand was clear that a campus should be mainly two things: trees and grass (fig. 77). "A campus is a place for trees and grass, nothing more," she wrote in a letter to Oberlin College. "And shrubs," she added, "but not in thickets."[4] This brief statement represents her first principle of campus landscaping.

As a rule, Farrand chose trees and shrubs that were native to the locale. This using of the vernacular was fundamental to Arts & Crafts philosophy. Use of local stone, local flora, and local craft was a hallmark of the movement. At Oberlin College in Ohio, Farrand planted "crabs and haws" (crabapples and hawthornes), the trees that the Prairie School of midwestern architects and landscape architects adopted as a mark of their approach, recommending them for their horizontal branching habits which reflected the horizontality of the prairie and enhanced its aesthetic qualities.

Farrand had her university nurseries specialize in plants native to or naturalized in the region. When recommending plants for any of her campuses, she recommended native flora "for long life." At Princeton she observed: "Red oaks and gum trees do particularly well in Princeton," and proceeded to make them the backbone of her campus plantings. But she never banished all others from campus use and liked to experiment by growing specimens from seeds given to a university from afar. However, the trees thus produced were used sparsely.

Generally, Farrand wanted deciduous trees for her campuses and she selected them for form. "Some of our new trees are developing to be poor types. . . . Remove and put in more vase-shaped trees."[5] Evergreens were used sparsely. In courtyards they tended to block the light. Interspersed with deciduous trees, they created the wrong effect.

> *Evergreen trees should be used with moderation. They appear as dark spots in deciduous plantations and while attractive now and again in winter they should not be over-emphasized. The controlling principle should be the use of the long-lived noble trees of the neighborhood, maple, oak, beech, ash, and so on, rather than to search for alien sorts which in the long run will be less successful and fit into the picture less easily.*[6]

The desire for simplicity and calm in her campus schemes meant that Farrand generally avoided using flowers. They required too much maintenance and had only a short-term effect.

> *Frankly, I don't believe we ought to go into rose growing in the Graduate Court. In the first place, it would mean beds for them which, as you know, would be rather disturbing to the general quiet of the scheme; and second it would mean a considerable amount of upkeep in the way of spraying and general care, and lastly most of the flowers would be in bloom while the students are away.*[7]

Spring-flowering bulbs, however, were allowed. "Self-renewing and needing little care, they add variety to the college courtyards; bulbs have been bought for many of the quadrangles and will, I hope, make a good show for themselves next spring."[8]

Farrand kept the center of the campus courtyard as free as possible. She wanted to give the students a central usable space for walking through, being in, or viewing from the rooms that surrounded it. Consequently, no fountains, statues, or trees occupied this center. Instead, she favored paths cutting through the grass (fig. 78). When a storm damaged the old elm in Yale's Saybrook Courtyard, she had it removed and vetoed its replacement.

Surrounding walls were to have unobstructed windows. A Princeton memo of 29 September 1934 says: "The barberries must be watched so that they do not encroach on the light of the windows." This principle was so important that Farrand either planted her trees off the walkways or trained them as wall plantings, a horticultural development she perfected and used extensively, particularly in Princeton. By wall plantings here, I do not mean vines placed on walls (though she used them too), but trees planted and then pruned to grow flat against the wall. While they resembled the espaliered fruit trees of medieval gardens, they were not fruit trees and therefore were not thinned to allow fruit to ripen against the warm stone. Instead, the foliage was allowed to form a dense, green mass on the wall.

The medieval parallel, however, is not fortuitous. The Romantic Move-

78. Paths at the New Quad, Graduate College Quadrangle, Princeton University, 1984. Photograph: Alan Ward.

ment rejected classicism and embraced the Gothic as the foundation of its new aesthetic. The Gothic tradition provided an alternative in countries such as England whose basic tradition did not stem from the Mediterranean and whose Christian background was more recent and did not evolve from classicism. To both the Romantic and the Arts & Crafts movements, the Christian Northern-European past offered the material for a new aesthetic that would surpass the one that had evolved from the culture of Greece and Rome. The resemblance to medieval courtyards was part of Farrand's objective.

The Arts & Crafts Movement found additional reasons to value the Gothic. The process by which Gothic buildings were constructed was more democratic and creative for the craftsmen involved than in the classic imperial tradition (in which buildings were used to represent the power of a city or an empire) or the industrialized, piecemeal approach (in which the makers lost all control over design of the object produced). Gothic building left the makers in control; sculptors could introduce individual pieces into an overall design, which allowed such freedom. Farrand used her wall plantings like the sculpted, crafted pieces in the Gothic edifice; each was a specific contribution to the design.

In her correspondence with Princeton, Farrand listed the trees she used for wall plantings:

Laburnums
White or pale pink double-flowering Peach
Five-leaf Aralia—"unusually attractive as a wall plant"
Korean dogwood (*Cornus kousa*)—"a very good wall plant"
Magnolia (*Magnolia kobus*)
Purple-leaved Hazel (*Corylus avellana*)
Ampelopsis periploca
Crabapples espaliered in a palmette form
Sourwood (*Oxydendrum arboreum*)

Many are still living and even flourishing on Princeton walls (figs. 79 & 80). Farrand also trained shrubs with long, sweeping branches which were strapped to the wall and either allowed to tumble down the wall or trained upward. Princeton and Yale still have many forsythias planted in this manner.

Farrand did not particularly like the ivy-covered halls of hallowed tradition and she said so at Oberlin:

79. Wall plantings at Princeton University, 1984. Photograph: Alan Ward.

> *I do strongly feel that our best wall planting for the future is going to be wall shrubs but . . . we can use the Boston Ivy . . . to make a complete screen to a hideous building.*

She proceeded there to remove the already-existing vines, not without some protest from the inhabitants:

> *Mr. Love seems much concerned at the complete removal of the creepers on the Administration Building and I am therefore writing him saying that this particular building is in my opinion too handsome to be muffled by a*

80. Wisteria and *Magnolia kobus* used as wall plantings at Princeton University, 1984. Photograph: Alan Ward.

ruffled screen of Boston Ivy, but that I would welcome well trained wall shrubs on its walls, bringing out rather than muffling its character. . . . Boston Ivy was meant to hide the ugly buildings.

To Mr. Love, the Oberlin secretary, she explained her viewpoint:

Frankly the Boston Ivy on the Administration Building is not a good enough plant to use on this handsome construction. Let us keep this by all means for hideous places like . . . the west side wall of the Carnegie Library. . . . If Boston Ivy had the architectural quality of English Ivy and made handsome pockets of shadow my grudge against it would not be so vicious.[9]

Farrand held ivies in high esteem only when they were combined to form a richly textured tapestry of different leaf sizes, shapes, and arbors. In her report to Oberlin dated 23 June 1939, she listed the ivies she would like to use. In all cases, she combined two or more together:

Virginia Creeper, English Ivy, Climbing Hydrangea, Trumpet Creeper, and certain types of Grape Vine are all adapted to the needs of Oberlin, and all of them cling to stone or stucco wall surfaces. Those which require wire or trellis training are also suitable, like certain climbing roses, Honeysuckles, Clematis, Actinidias, etc. This climbing plant material if well trained and controlled will beautify wall surfaces without unduly encumbering them and will accent the vertical lines without muffling the foundation spring line, or occupying space needed for traffic.[10]

After selecting native trees, Farrand chose plants that were most interesting during fall, winter, and spring. She rejected those that peaked in summer when the students were away. A letter to Yale's comptroller, Thomas Farnam, tells him what plants she is choosing for the Yale campus and why: "The planting should be at its best in the spring and autumn, so . . . spring-flowering trees and shrubs and those which color well in the autumn have been selected in preference to summer-flowering sorts." She had selected "dogwood, some of the native thorns [hawthorns], coronillas, high-bush

XI. The landscape of a Gothic quadrangle at Branford College, Harkness Memorial Quadrangle, Yale University, 1984. Photograph: Kenneth Champlin.

XII. Yew-bordered walk into the Princeton University campus from the railroad station, 1984. Photograph: Alan Ward.

XIII. York Street by the Harkness Quadrangle, Yale University; a moat bordering the building is planted with trees and shrubs. Photograph: Alan Ward.

XIV. The White House garden designed by Farrand. Courtesy of University of California, Berkeley; Department of Landscape Architecture; Documents Collection.

XV. California poppies in the meadow of the Santa Barbara Botanic Garden. Photograph: Les Smith.

blueberries, the shining sumac, a few barberries, and some of the early-flowering crabapples."[11] In the previously mentioned Oberlin College report she repeated this theme:

> *The seasons when the college is most used indicate the choice of plant material. The use of the local flora should predominate, at least for material of long life. . . . As the college is mainly used during the leafless months of the year, it should be constantly borne in mind that colour of autumn foliage, character or shape of winter bark and branching, and beauty of spring flowering should control choice of plant material.*

The Shaping of the Ground: Walks, Steps, and Contours

Farrand gave a lot of attention to the design of roads and walks and of steps along these walks, and to the shaping of the ground around walks and buildings. While this issue may appear to be a technical one—of interest only to experts—it is not. A great part of the pleasure derived from traversing a landscape relates to the way one travels through it. Is the route comfortable or too steep? Does it offer a pleasant view? Is it too circuitous, too narrow, too full of interruptions? How do you approach a building? Does it seem overbearing, stark, out of place? All these matters were crucial to Farrand's campus designs, and this was an area in which she exhibited extraordinary talent. The plan for the Yale Freshman Quadrangle (fig. 81) shows how she redesigned walks to make them as convenient and straight as possible between gates and entrances.

Farrand traversed and carefully studied the campus site for direct approaches, good views, comfort, and walking ease. Then she contoured, graded, and made clear lines of access and approach to the different buildings on the campus. Paths were constructed above ground level for good drainage. At Princeton, she recommended that paths be set two inches above the sod.[12]

Some plantings took the form of walks, for example the Russell Memorial Walk designed for the Princeton Garden Club (to the great satisfaction of club members from the university) through existing woods on the edge of the Princeton campus. Farrand added viburnums—"whatever tall growing types are available"—throughout the years to border the walk.[13] She also designed a fence and entrance steps and placed a large boulder with a memorial plaque at the entrance. What remains of this walk is now half-forgotten and encroached upon by new building. The Butler Memorial Walk, close by, is in slightly better condition.

Farrand also worked very hard at designing appropriate grade levels around a building, adjusting contours to establish a better relation between a building and the ground it stood on. In one major disagreement with Ralph Adams Cram at Princeton, she clearly was right and the architect wrong. The case involved the approach to the Graduate College.

Farrand incurred Cram's wrath by creating a low terrace where he wanted a sloping lawn. However, her reason—that a terrace wall would give added visual support to the building, "replacing the weak impermanent line

81. The Freshman Quadrangle plan for Yale University. Courtesy of University of California, Berkeley; Department of Landscape Architecture; Documents Collection.

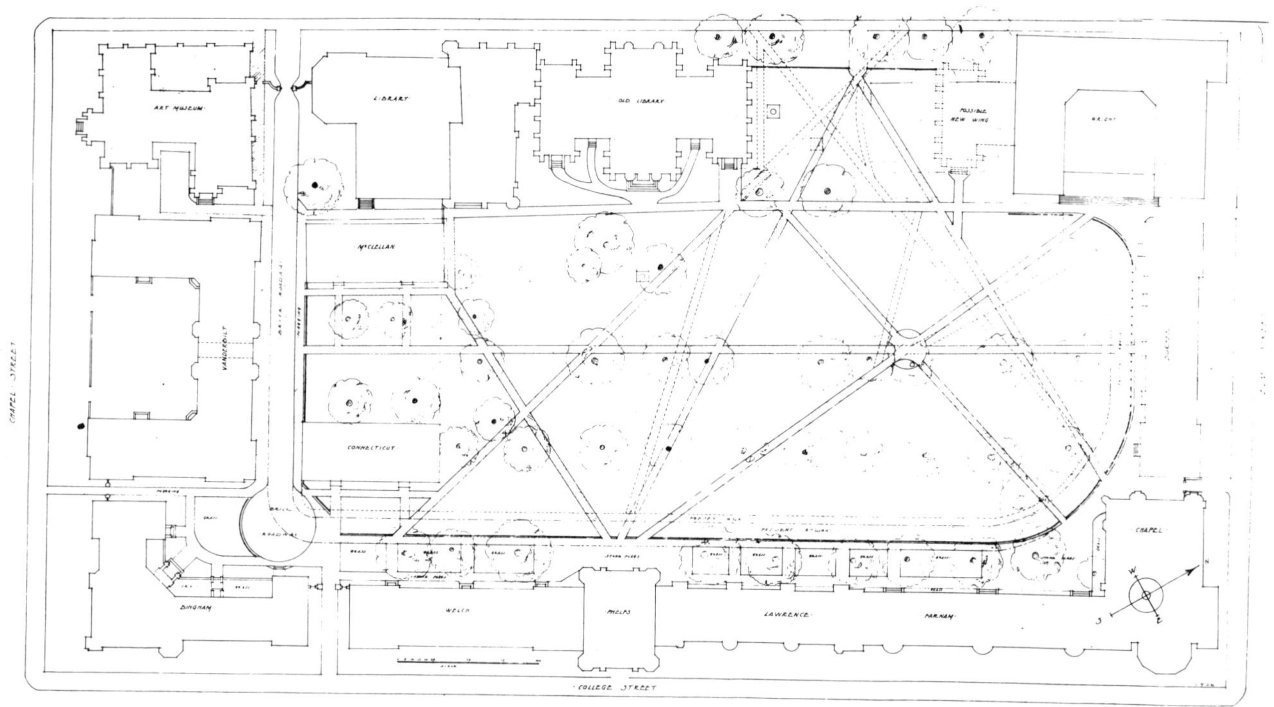

of a grassy bank"—was correct. One look at the Graduate College terrace today reveals that a grassy slope would have been overwhelmed by the massive buildings.

In matters of this sort, Farrand seems to have gained the confidence of the universities she worked with, for she was always given the authority to modify the grades after the architects or engineers had finished setting them.

> *I stopped . . . on my way back . . . to consult with Mr. Klauder [the architect] with regard to the grades surrounding the new Peabody Museum [at Yale]. We carefully considered the whole question and we agree that the grade at the building should be forty which means a raise of two feet from the grade of thirty-eight originally proposed. I ventured to make some suggestions to Mr. Klauder with regard to providing open spaces around the building and the possible re-spacing of certain areas in order to allow planting space at the strategic points. Mr. Klauder quite saw the advisability of certain of these suggestions and kindly said he would see that these small changes were made.*[14]

And from the California Institute of Technology, the chairman of the Buildings and Grounds Committee wrote her: "The levels have been arranged, as you doubtless know, in accordance with your recommendations, although the architects strongly urged a different plan."[15]

Exterior steps were an essential part of the walks, and Farrand adopted a basic principle for dealing with them: "The steps . . . should be divided into two or three runs. The risers not over 6 inches and treads not less than 12 inches. If possible 14 inch treads and 5½ inch risers. . . . Largeness and generous proportion and scale should be maintained in the design."[16]

A final detail, adding to campus comfort and incorporated as part of her courtyard and walk designs, was the placement of benches. "Mrs. Farrand . . . reminded Mr. MacMillan [at Princeton] that seats, benches and so on, would be desirable to add to the various dormitories and courts as they have proved popular and good looking at Yale and Chicago."[17] To place them, she studied student preferences. "One of the new 1937 teak benches was to be placed on the upper terrace of the south court and watched as to where the students found it most attractive."[18]

For those thinking that security issues were completely different in the past and that benches were loosely placed on a college campus, the 1938 notes quickly dispel the notion. Disappearing campus benches, the bane of landscapers today, "walked away" then too:

> *It was agreed that the . . . new teak bench should be placed in the north court and a possible position picked out by Mr. Clark and Mrs. Farrand. The bench . . . is to be attached to a couple of heavy wooden or concrete posts sunk in the ground to which the bench is to be screwed by an iron at the diagonal front and back legs.*[19]

Developing Campus Nurseries

Farrand campaigned to establish plant nurseries at each of her campuses, and her efforts relate to a basic philosophy of campus planting. To university officials she justified her incessant drive in very pragmatic terms: the college could grow its own plants rather than buy them commercially, thus getting better plants for less money and obtaining varieties not commonly available. But to Farrand, the nursery was much more.

This central, critical element of Farrand's thinking reflected a philosophy that again stemmed from the Arts & Crafts Movement. For her and other practitioners, landscaping was not simply a matter of purchasing and arranging plants but rather of actively creating an environment. This process included obtaining better species and growing them in the soil and climate where they would be living; trying new species grown from seed; experimenting with varieties; and making new plant discoveries.

The Arts & Crafts Movement criticized the industrial process that divorced the designer from the production of the object designed. In landscape, purchasing all plants from a commercial nursery paralleled that process. William Robinson and Gertrude Jekyll, major figures of the Arts & Crafts Movement in landscape, for example, attacked the Victorian practice of "bedding out," i.e. regularly putting quantities of plants purchased or grown elsewhere in planting beds instead of growing plants in place. One of the most moving statements in Farrand's Princeton planting notes refers to this involvement in caring for plants: "Mrs. Farrand rejoices with Mr.

Clark [the head gardener] in seeing that the two big recently moved *Taxus gracilis* were still living and apparently growing gaily."[20]

Farrand obtained seeds from many horticultural sources, such as the Royal Horticultural Society, the Arnold Arboretum, the Morton Arboretum, and the New York and Edinburgh botanical gardens. From them, she grew many of the trees and bushes with which she at first planted her campuses. Later, when Princeton, Yale, and Chicago had established nurseries, she encouraged them to exchange seeds and plants. While this approach seems logical, it is certainly rare at universities today. Of the nurseries Farrand created, only Princeton's still remains, and it is much smaller in scale and scope than the original.

Farrand believed that establishing a nursery related to the educational function of the university in fundamental ways: landscape practices would contribute knowledge of plants and would link departments at the university, such as Botany and Forestry, where such knowledge could be put to use for the university's own purposes. Her ultimate aim, however, was only imperfectly achieved and it never received recognition. She wanted each campus to be a museum of trees, native or natural to the region, that would educate students to the plants around them. The nursery made the landscape "site specific," linking it to the environment through plants which grew best there.

> *Under the direction of Mrs. Farrand, different parts of the University grounds as a whole are being utilized for the display of different groups of woody plants. It has been suggested also that the plantings at the [Botanical] Garden might best be made with a view to bringing out the distribution of plants in relation to various features of environment, i.e. with reference to their ecological relations.*[21]

Farrand worked for many years at each campus to get a nursery established. Her justification to university officials remained pragmatic: "Essential that there be a nursery started as buying oversized material is expensive."[22] Once a nursery had been started, she encouraged the principal gardeners to visit horticultural institutions and each other's campuses, to correspond with seed suppliers, and to subscribe to horticultural journals.

This way, they would keep abreast of horticultural news and observe others growing plants. Mr. Peberdy from Yale visited Princeton to inspect the wall-training of plants.[23] James Clark, Princeton's head gardener, wanted Yale's recipe for rhododendron fertilizer and, in turn, sent seedling azaleas.[24] Thus the gardener practiced a creative occupation very much in keeping with the Arts & Crafts spirit; he was not reduced to carting plants and cleaning. And Farrand herself constantly visited other places for her own education. In 1933 she went to Oxford and Cambridge "to learn a little from the work there that can be useful at Princeton."[25]

By the end of her career, Farrand had created her own "university of campus landscaping" by getting all those under her direction to collaborate in one large exchange and in many plant experiments. Memos indicate that these efforts were extraneous to her official commissions; she made them because they embodied her landscape philosophy.

Though Farrand established her first nursery at Princeton, she did not write about it until she began corresponding with Yale. In fact, she wrote relatively little. Only during her later campus jobs (from the early 1920s through the 1930s) did she begin describing her general approach on paper, and then mainly in correspondence with university officials. In the 5 July 1922 Yale nursery proposal, for example, she explained the financial operation of the university nursery using examples from the other universities: "[The] university is to be charged what it used and credited with the labor it employed in it. This has proved a profitable undertaking for Princeton University."[26]

After establishing nurseries at Princeton, Yale, and Chicago, Farrand had each specialize in a few different plants and then supply the other campuses with them. Princeton specialized in different magnolias, in varieties of forsythia, and in Ericaceae (heathers), also azaleas and rhododendron. Yale experimented with "magnolias, ericads, and certain broad-leaved evergreens."[27] A memo following one of Farrand's Princeton visits reports: "Three eastern colleges with which Mrs. Farrand is associated are all willing to share their nursery material and a list has been made to circulate among others."[28]

The exchange of plants, people, and knowledge was not confined to her university clients. Farrand also had private clients purchase surplus plants from university nurseries. And the Royal Horticultural Society sent her seeds of rare shrubs to try at Yale and Princeton and asked her to send the results to the Director of Experimental Gardens at Wisley as a courtesy.[29]

At Chicago, she proposed starting the university's nursery with plants which might be obtained from the Rochester City Parks or the Morton Arboretum. If the university could not obtain them there, she suggested it then try Princeton's or Yale's nursery. The university's notes summarizing one of her visits are indicative of her practical approach:

> *Mrs. Farrand also suggested we might be able to negotiate an exchange of plants with both Princeton and Yale. For this we are to write to Mr. Crafton Peberdy and Mr. James Clark, their respective head gardeners. She recommended we provide an area large enough to grow 1500 shrubs and trees, 4,000–5,000 ground covers (space 150 × 100 feet) and . . . request an area in Botany gardens. Comparative ground expenditures from Princeton/Yale would be helpful in justifying an increase in our grounds budget. She is planning to compose a lecture on the value of landscape beauty to student life to be given at cultural classes at the various universities.*[30]

As a matter of fact, Farrand began her job at the University of Chicago with a gift of plants from the nursery she had started at Yale:

> *When the Trustees of the University of Chicago decided to ask me to do the planting around the Sunny Gymnasium, it occurred to me to write to my assistant at Yale asking whether we could spare some of our big Forsythia from Yale, and that the carload may be filled with other shrubs in order to make the full load. Fortified by this information, I asked Mr. Thomas W. Farnam, the Associate Treasurer and Comptroller of the University, whether he felt this gift to the University of Chicago might be possible, and he has today sent me word that the Prudential Committee of Yale, at a recent meeting "expressed a keen desire to cooperate with you in making a gift of Forsythia to the University of Chicago." I have at once sent Mr. Farnam my own personal hearty thanks and feel sure that you will either wish to*

send him a message by me, or communicate with him directly thanking him for the offer which the Prudential Committee has so generously made.[31]

According to a Chicago correspondent, "the forsythia she took here fifty-five years ago continues to bloom and flourish."[32]

Farrand's insistence on the value of establishing nurseries needs to be analyzed in a larger context because it was such an important element in her theory of landscaping. She was not unique in her efforts. Frederick Law Olmsted had attempted to do something similar. At Stanford, he wanted to create an arboretum containing representative trees of the local and similar climates. At Biltmore, the large Vanderbilt estate in North Carolina that was the last of his major works, he developed the idea even further. Not only was a major arboretum or collection of trees to be planted on the thousands of acres comprising the estate, but scientific foresting would also take place, providing wood and making the project self-sustaining. The interest in producing trees, reforesting, and using native plants was a general part of the late-nineteenth-century landscape movement and owed much of its impetus to people like Professor Othniel C. Marsh who left his money for the botanic garden at Yale. Arts & Crafts Movement ideas were imbedded in this approach. But Olmsted's efforts at Stanford and his plans for Biltmore did not work out exactly as intended. Beatrix Farrand's nurseries, however, succeeded, serving their respective campuses for many decades.

THE PROFESSIONAL AT WORK

Beatrix Jones Farrand (fig. 82) ran a professional practice from the first, though in the field of landscape design, the professional office as we know it today was just emerging when she started her practice in the late 1890s. By the late 1920s, her system and methods for field and office work were highly developed. Her professionalism was also reflected in the fact that she was one of the seven founding members of the American Society of Landscape Architects.

The many years of involvement with each campus, the many campuses and the massive correspondence with each, plus the field visits and the copious memos which accompanied each visit, make it obvious that Beatrix

82. Beatrix Farrand; undated photograph probably taken in the 1920s or early 1930s. Courtesy of University of California, Berkeley; Department of Landscape Architecture; Documents Collection.

Farrand was not a lone practitioner working out of a desk. In fact she had a professional office, and to understand her campus work we need to see how that work was done. The professional landscape office is an intrinsic part of that story.

Women who are new or rare in a professional world have always had to contend with the issue of forms of address in attempting to establish themselves professionally. "Will you see that when my name goes on the rolls that I am put down as Beatrix Farrand without any qualifying Mr. or Mrs. or Miss, as I regard Beatrix Farrand as a sort of trade name."[33] On 18 October 1922 she made this request of Yale after getting official confirmation of her appointment to landscape the Harkness Memorial Quadrangle. To no avail. It will come as no surprise that, despite many such requests, she never succeeded in being addressed as anything but Mrs. Farrand.

> *Dear Mrs. Farrand:*
>
> *I am glad to enclose herewith our check for $180 in payment of your bill recently rendered. I am sorry that the check was made out to Mrs. Beatrix Farrand rather than to the more professional style of Beatrix Farrand, but the check was made before I noticed it. I trust the paper will still be worth face value to you.*[34]

It was clearly impossible for a lone individual to bring about change.

Women professionals of this period usually worked for others, or, if they had their own offices, were often lone practitioners with an occasional helper. Beatrix Farrand had an office of four to six people. She employed mostly women, some of whom eventually established their own practices. Ruth Havey, who took over the landscaping at Dumbarton Oaks when Farrand retired, was one of them. She has given some valuable details about Farrand's working habits and her method of running the office.

> *I would bring the drawings being developed at the office and get on the train in New York and meet her on the train. She was usually on her way to do fieldwork in one of the jobs. We would review the plans, she would make suggestions and critiques or changes. As soon as the review was finished, I would get off at the next station, wherever that may be, and take a train back to New York.*[35]

Farrand worked on trains because of her intense field work at each site and because she lived in New Haven, and later California, but maintained her principal office in New York. Moreover, she moved her practice to Bar Harbor, Maine in late spring and returned it to New York City in the fall. The Bar Harbor base in summer handled all the commissions for gardens located in Maine, an important resort area in the 1920s and the location of her family's summer home and those of many of her clients.

After her husband, Yale historian Max Farrand, became director of the Huntington Library in San Marino, Farrand spent the winter months in California. She added a few California jobs to her practice but never had enough California commissions to open a full-fledged operation there, so she maintained her New York office. Farrand's use of traveling time for working was highly efficient, given the amount of commuting she did as a way of life.

Another mark of her professionalism is the care and attention given to billings. She wanted to insure that the services rendered would be considered those of a professional, not those of an amateur doing work as a volunteer, a category in which women's work was frequently placed by institutions. Her work for the California Institute of Technology is a good case in point. She was asked in 1932 to give advice on the landscaping of the institute, which she did without charge. She suggested some changes and offered to oversee them, again without charge, though she asked payment for the laborers' time and a small sum for planting material. It was clear that she was trying to obtain a commission as landscape consultant to the institute. Though the director of the institute, Robert Millikan, seems to have been interested in bringing expertise to the institute's landscaping, the chairman of the Buildings and Grounds Committee was not, and he decided that his committee would specify when and what to plant, with occasional advice, free if possible, from Beatrix Farrand. How she tried to change her generously given advice into a professional service—yet rendered without cost to the institution—is the mark of a high professional intent:

> *As you know, Mr. Robinson and I discussed the question of my helping the appearance of the buildings and he and I agreed that in order to accomplish what was then in mind my time would be given freely to carry out the early*

projects. When the work increased to the point when it consumed a much greater amount of my time, an account was sent as a matter of professional practice, which was accompanied by a cheque as a present to the Institute so that my work would not mean a cost to the Institute. The point involved is not one of compensation but affecting professional relations and accepted customs. If the Institute feels it needs help in landscape construction from me or anyone else, it might prevent complications if a small salary or fee could be arranged; perhaps an annual one of one hundred dollars and an allowance of fifty dollars for expenses, on the understanding that no commitment was made involving more than six months or a year at a time.[36]

Given that she had started her services in 1928, it appears she had considerable patience. The letter above was written in 1938.

The response to her repeated requests for professional recognition had been not to offer her a position as a landscape consultant but to make her an Associate of the institute, which she declined in the same letter to Robert Millikan in the following way:

Our talk a few days ago has been often in mind and it complimented and flattered me that you should have made the suggestion upon which we touched. It is nice to know that one is wanted and for me the association would be an honourable one, but I do not feel it possible to accept as there would be an ever present consciousness of not having a real right to be one of the group. It would never seem quite fair to benefit from the result of a kindly thought on your part, as it would be, in a way, definitely sailing under false financial colours.[37]

But to the chairman of the Committee on Buildings and Grounds she was very direct and precise on her unhappiness at her status:

In talking with you recently, it was clear to me that no decision had as yet been reached with regard to my professional relations with the California Institute. As you have doubtless realized, I am not happy in the work as my present half-charitable, half-amateur status is not satisfactory. My position at the Institute is an anomalous one, and quite different from my relations with other institutions. Suggestions made are frequently changed in what seem to me essential details, and responsibility for outdoor design lies in many different hands. It appears to me more professionally dignified to stop working at the Institute until the Committee decides where or not it intends to employ me professionally.[38]

It seems that Farrand did succeed in being professionally consulted on a one-time consulting charge basis, as per a letter dated 17 October 1938. On the other hand there does not appear to be more than this one further consultation.

The attempt to be treated as a professional revealed in this set of exchanges with the California Institute of Technology, as well as the effort to have her full name used without the marital-status form of address, both reflect how clearly Farrand saw the importance of obtaining the respect due a professional, particularly in her relations with university officials.

Those interested in Farrand often ask if she was more a field person—actually designing on the ground, pointing here and there to place the plants—than a designer on paper. Though Farrand put a lot of stock in what she saw and visualized on the site, she based her plans on detailed land surveys that she carefully studied at the beginning of each job. The survey, in fact, is the most prominent plan in every job folder in the University of California's collection of her files at Berkeley. She clearly worked from these surveys, visualizing the design in three dimensions.

Her review of a design for a bench shows us another aspect of her landscape practice that hardly fits the "point-and-place" category:

I suggested to Miss Havey that we have a second bar across the back of [the] seat rather than the series of panels (back of this seat too heavy). Draw it to Miss Baker's attention and ask her to show these drawings to me together with a tracing of the back with three bars as originally planned but modified in spacing and size.[39]

Proof of the care and attention Farrand gave to garden furnishings and walkways lies in the drawing folders for specific jobs (also in the University of California collection). Her designs were drawn on a very large scale: 1:1, full-scale; or 1:2, half-scale. This forced her staff to work at a level of subtle detail. Steps, walk-widths, paving patterns, benches, gates, and moldings were all drawn at these large scales, and much office time must have been spent in producing them. (An example of a full-size detail of a bench for the University of Chicago is reproduced in figure 83.) In addition, many layouts of walks and steps were made on coarse paper, some at actual size. Elsewhere I have described the careful dummying-up or model-making of the dimensions of paths and steps.[40] All the examples I have seen show that Farrand gave the same care to every aspect of landscape design that she did to planting.

Farrand's field-work at the different campuses was painstaking and methodical. James Clark, the head gardener at Princeton who worked with her for over thirty years, has told about her inspection visits to Princeton—an average of three a year. On the first day of each of her two-day inspections, she would review all the work requested at her last visit. On the second day, she would check the whole campus and list the items needing attention (removal, pruning or new planting, new walks, etc.). She then would have the head gardener write a detailed memorandum, file one copy, and send the other to her. Fortunately, these have been preserved at Princeton. Correspondence with officialdom of other campuses indicates that she used the same method; however the memoranda are missing and we cannot reconstruct her working habits in the same detail for other campuses.

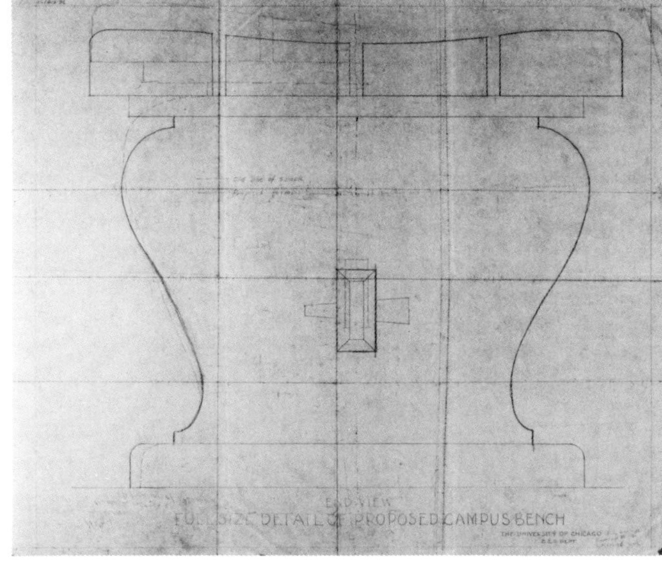

83. Full-scale drawing of a bench for the University of Chicago. Courtesy of University of California, Berkeley; Department of Landscape Architecture; Documents Collection.

THE WORK AT SPECIFIC CAMPUSES

Princeton University (1912–1943)

The best way to understand Farrand's working methods and her principles of landscape design is to follow her activity at one campus in detail. Princeton has been chosen for this purpose for three reasons. Princeton was her first campus project and she worked there over a longer period of time than at any other public institution. Moreover, her involvement with Princeton can be completely reconstructed because the records of her visits are complete and, with the planting memos, are preserved in the archives at the Seeley Mudd Library. These documents make it possible to see her campus design take shape. Finally, on no other campus is so much of her landscape still visible and, in parts, even flourishing. A glance at a current Princeton University map which has the areas landscaped by Farrand crosshatched (fig. 84) shows how much of the campus is hers, though others have worked on it at a later date. Thirty-odd years of work leave a mark, and Farrand's is a high level of landscaping. Thanks to Farrand, Princeton has a particularly good mix of natural and designed settings, and a feeling of settled calm.

As mentioned earlier, Farrand first came to Princeton in 1912 to design the grounds for its new Graduate College. She was thirty years old. Farrand had already designed several private gardens though not yet her major ones, and probably she was not all that well known. How did she, a woman, get the commission for this male college? Being a founding member of the group that professionalized landscape architecture must have helped. But more importantly, she may well have been recommended by Charles Sprague Sargent, her former teacher and the director of the Arnold Arboretum at Harvard. Sargent had sent to Dean West, the dean of the new Graduate College and the principal proponent at Princeton of the ideas this new complex of buildings represented, two cedars of Lebanon. They had been grown at the Arnold Arboretum from seeds gathered in the Cilician Mountains. Farrand had been one of Sargent's favorite pupils, and he could expect that she would spread important horticultural ideas while working at the university. Sargent very possibly sent her to West. Certainly, he later helped in her

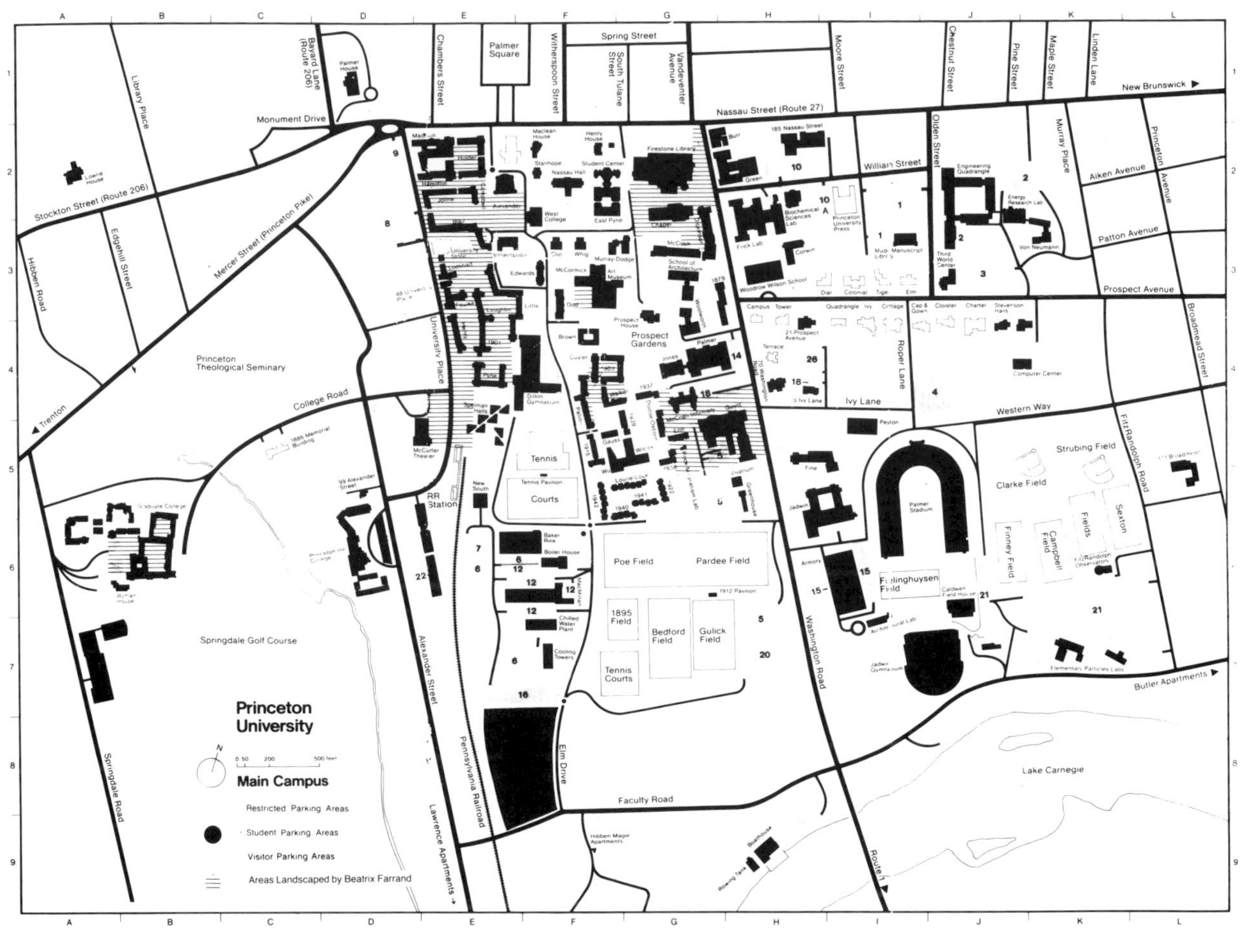

84. Map of Princeton University today; areas landscaped by Farrand are crosshatched.

campus work, sending seeds to the university and having the head gardener come up to the arboretum for cuttings or seeds.

When Farrand (then Jones) came to Princeton, her fee was fifty dollars a day, which today translates into five hundred dollars a day—the fee of an established professional.

> *In regard to the terms of payment, my charges are fifty dollars a day and my travelling expenses. Work done in the office is paid for at the same rate; thus a complicated plan might require four or five days to complete and a rough sketch half a day; office expense such as telegrams, etc. and writing*

of specifications is charged to the client at the same rate at which I pay for it; no percentage of any kind is charged on anything.[41]

While designing the Graduate College, she visited six times a year; later she averaged two or three visits yearly. Yet in those few days she worked quickly and accomplished a great deal. Professor Willard Thorpe, who taught anthropology at Princeton, is related by marriage to Beatrix Farrand (his wife being Max Farrand's niece). He described how she had worked on a garden design she did for him during her Princeton years. The quickness of mind she displayed doubtless characterized also her approach to his institution.

She came and walked around our site for half an hour, then came back in and gave us a general layout, telling us what plants we should put in, in what form, and where they should go; all of which we did. The only thing we didn't do was to open a vista in the wood behind the house—one of her final suggestions. Rumors of a shopping center behind the woods made us hold off on this, fortunately, because the shopping center got built. But in half an hour she had a very clear picture in her mind.[42]

Farrand's relations with Princeton were somewhat more formal. After visiting the Princeton grounds, she wrote a report[43] and outlined her proposals. She thought the following points were primary, and the first the most important:

CONNECTING OF THE GRADUATE COLLEGE TO THE UNIVERSITY CAMPUS.

The map shows that the College is removed to the west from the rest of the campus. Thus connecting it by pleasurable and efficient walks was the first order of business. Adequate and dignified road and footpath connections were needed for direct, convenient, and quiet access to the University Library, the Chemical Laboratories, and other points.

ROADS AND FOOTPATHS. *It is suggested that only indispensable roads and paths be constructed at present, leaving future developments to be indicated by the necessities of the travel itself; thus, in the quadrangle only the walks adjacent to the buildings and those communicating with the various entries, have been shown, in the hope that it may be possible to preserve unbroken the stretch of grass in the middle of the enclosure.* Farrand also explained why she proposed moving existing roads and gave reasons for the way she had designed the new ones. The beautiful approach to the campus from the railroad station along a direct planted walk can be seen in plate XII.

BUILDING TO BE MOVED. The golf clubhouse was too close to the Graduate College.

PLANTING. She suggested that most plantings be in borders that would both follow the walks and surround the edges of the Graduate College. Most of the plants were to be trees, not shrubs. The trees to be planted first were the Red Oak (*Quercus rubra*), Basswood (*Tilia americana*), Sugar Maple (*Acer saccharum*), Buttonwood (*Platanus occidentalis*), Sweet Gum (*Liquidambar styraciflua*), and Tulip tree (*Liriodendron tulipifera*), with occasional masses of Dogwood (*Cornus florida*).

PLANTING AROUND THE BUILDINGS. *As the large buildings are so dignified in character and so large in size, the planting should be kept simple in all respects. Within the quadrangle only, creepers and wall shrubs should be used, as free standing shrubs would tend to destroy the impression of quiet which the buildings themselves give. The wall planting in the quadrangle should be partly evergreen in character. In all the planting design it has been kept in mind that the planting should look its best between the months of October and June, and therefore evergreens both broad leaved and coniferous should be incorporated in the scheme. On the north side of the buildings a somewhat heavy plantation has been shown, as there are considerable changes of grade which can be masked by planting.*

TERRACE AND ENTRANCE COURT. Farrand surrounded the approach to the Graduate College with a wall, which created an entrance court that continued in front of Cleveland Tower, *making a broad terrace, out of which Cleveland Tower will rise, and giving a quiet base to the line of buildings.*

In this initial report, Farrand gave only some general ideas about the planting, though she was specific about keeping courtyards clear and already was talking about wall planting. By December 27th of the following year, roads had been laid out, the clubhouse issue was settled, and the contouring and terracing had been completed. She then sent a specific and detailed report[44] that set forth the principles that became the hallmarks of her landscape planting. The note about native trees was sounded as the very first item.

> *The use of trees growing naturally in the district and under like conditions is strongly recommended, and of these the varieties should be chosen which have proved themselves long lived and suited to endure the local conditions of moisture and soil.*

Next came the strictures guiding plant selection.

> *The broad general principle is suggested that deciduous trees be used for the main planting on the Campus, for the reason that trees that shed their leaves give shade when shade is required and do not occupy as much ground space as properly grown evergreens. A conifer when its lower branches are pruned, in order to reduce the space it occupied, loses a large part of its beauty, as is proved by the appearance of old Norway spruces or hemlocks which have been shorn of their lower branches in order to give light on the ground below. Deciduous trees, when used, should be chosen of varieties which do not branch low. Where evergreen tree planting is used, it should be large masses. In this way, evergreens are effective in colour and substance, whereas if planted singly, they give a spotty effect and destroy any feeling of unity or repose in the general planting scheme. The general principle is, therefore, suggested that evergreen trees be used only in certain carefully considered places for large mass planting; but that the general scheme for the planting on the Campus should be deciduous.*

However inside the courtyard she wanted evergreens. And she had very specific ideas for wall plantings. She proposed:

that the buildings be covered in patches, not solidly, with masses of ivy, in several different varieties, and varied by masses of Euonymus radicans *(the broad-leaved variety), and by an occasional wall shrub which will give colour and change of texture for the spring and autumn. The planting around the buildings should be sparingly done in most cases, merely emphasizing the architectural lines and leaving the best of these features free to be seen. Where a building of an older type does not coincide in character with those of a later development, heavier planting could be used, which, while not hiding it completely, would apparently bring it more in harmony with the general scheme.*

Finally, she formally proposed the establishment of a nursery. For it, she recommended a piece of ground south of the Vivarium to be used for raising plants which could not be obtained from nurseries in large size and would be used in later plantings. She added a list of these trees and shrubs, including sizes and approximate prices. Later, when the nursery had outgrown its first position, she suggested that the trees and shrubs be transferred to the plot immediately next to it. Thus the nursery could expand yet remain in a central place.

According to Farrand, an expenditure of a thousand dollars would start a good nursery that would last for several years. She advised purchasing for it only a few deciduous trees, in small sizes for a small amount of money. Larger trees, while they might be useful, were more costly to purchase and to care for. The list below, while not long, would be ample both for the plantings around the buildings and for starting some large evergreen groups.

CONIFERS

Pseudotsuga mucronata (Douglas Spruce)
Tsuga canadensis (Hemlock)
Tsuga caroliniana (Carolina Hemlock)
Pinus strobus (White Pine)
Juniperus virginiana (Red Cedar)

DWARF CONIFERS

Pinus mughus (Dwarf Pine)
Chamaecyparis (Retinospora), vars. pisifera, plumosa, and squarrosa (Japanese Cypress)
Taxus cuspidata, var. brevifolia (Japanese Yew)
Taxus baccata, var. repandens (English Yew)

BROAD-LEAVED EVERGREEN SHRUBS

Abelia floribunda
Andromeda floribunda
Andromeda japonica
Buxus sempervirens (Box)
Pyracantha coccinea (Evergreen Thorn)
Euonymus japonicus
Ilex glabra (Ink Berry)
Ilex crenata (Japanese Holly)
Leucothoe catesbaei (Drooping Andromeda)
Rhododendron, hybrid varieties

From this report and the earlier one, we see that even on her first campus job, Farrand had a well-defined philosophy and a thorough approach to campus planting. By the time she began work on her Yale commission in 1922, she had tested the ideas and found that they worked. Thus she continued along the general lines she had here laid out, enriching each new job with variants and different native materials.

In her Princeton proposals, Farrand presented not just a scheme for the Graduate College, but for the whole campus. Whether she was extending the limits of her commission or working at the request of the university, we do not know. By 1915, however, she had been named Supervising Landscape Architect for Princeton University, a position comparable to one created in architecture for Ralph Adams Cram in 1905. In this position, Farrand gave the campus landscape a continuity and unity of purpose. Under her, Princeton became one of the best landscaped campuses in the United States. But her labors were not without difficulty.

Cram, the architect with whom she had to work at Princeton, was far from a pillar of support.

I am very strongly of the opinion that the landscape treatment around a given building should be determined by the architect thereof, as he must have necessarily visualized the whole composition, and from different points of view, as he worked out his plans; no landscape gardener, however competent, can be expected to see the thing as he sees it, the more so, in that the landscape gardener enters the premises late in the game and can hardly do more than acquire superficial impressions. . . . When it comes to the preparation of the soil, the selection of trees and shrubs, planting, etc. the landscape gardener is invaluable and is working on his own grounds. I make these points at this time in explanation of the fact that I cannot approve all the details of Miss Jones' [i.e. Farrand's] scheme.[45]

Among other things, Cram objected to Farrand's roads.

The new roads on the plan are to a great extent curvelinear and are too frequently double curves. I do not think these are as acceptable now as they were held to be ten years ago, and for my own part I prefer straight runs and unmechanical curves. I take particular exception to the carriage entrance and service entrance to the Dean's house.

He also objected to the paths and the planting that bordered them.

I cannot feel that Miss Jones' massing of trees and shrubbery is what it should be. She seems to have confined herself almost exclusively to borders for roads and paths, while she has left no vistas through.

And to the choice of materials.

My first impression is that the thicket of pines and hemlocks as shown would be most objectionable as it would, in time, practically cut off the entire view of the east side of the Graduate College from the main line of approach. This is the most important "prospect" of the buildings, and I should consider it unfortunate if they were masked so completely at this point.

Cram invoked Oxford and Cambridge as the source of his own landscaping scheme. He said that he had tried to keep entirely clear of the "old landscape architecture of a generation ago," perhaps referring to Olmsted. At any rate, Cram said he aimed for the effect of an English Park, though how that tied in with Oxford and Cambridge, which did not look like parks, is not clear.

Nor was Cram alone at Princeton in his criticism of Farrand. One administrator, responding to an inquiry about Farrand's abilities, wrote in the following fashion to a correspondent who was thinking of hiring her to landscape the grounds of a boys school in Philadelphia:[46]

> *While Mrs. Farrand is a good Landscape Gardener, and has done some very commendable work for us, I would have a very definite understanding with regard to what she is to do and the times at which you would expect to have her services. I am sounding this note of warning because she is very busy and in addition, I fear combines too much pleasure with business. In other words, I do not believe she has that sense of responsibility toward her clients, which, looking at it from a purely business standpoint, I think any one who engages to do a piece of work should have.*
>
> *I would not entrust to her any large grading jobs or any road building. Our experience with her on this kind of work has not been satisfactory. She has all the assurance in the world and will tackle anything, but like every one else, she has her limitations.*
>
> *She charges for her services, $50.00 per day and expenses, and that is the basis on which she works for us. Kindly treat what I have said as confidential.*

She did not get the job.

These letters are indicative of the kinds of resistance that a woman professional would have encountered when working in the public realm. That Farrand should have prevailed against such entrenched interests must indicate a high degree of tact as well as rightness and persistence on her part.

During the succeeding years at Princeton, Farrand filled in the details of the landscape and changed plants. Trees planted in 1914 were thinned in the 1920s. The nursery was expanded. Experiments in pruning and propagating became important. In the first decade, Farrand's reports contain detailed descriptions of trees to be planted. She developed a long list of those that should *not* be planted and explained why. A corresponding list of favored trees—developed subsequent to the list in her initial report—also contained reasons for using them.

By the 1920s, Farrand began to take full advantage of the Princeton climate, in which both northern and southern trees could thrive. Southern transplants, like the magnolia, hugged the walls exposed to the southern sun.

Farrand always insisted that native trees be used before exotic, imported ones. Therefore, she said "no" to the Norwegian maple.

> *They have not been chosen among the desireable varieties, as they do not colour well in the autumn and they are awkward and stiff in shape for many years. The European Sycamore Maple* (Acer pseudo-platanus) *should also be classed with the Norway Maple, as well as the European Cork Maple* (Acer campestris) *and all the cut-leaved and purple-leaved varieties of these trees. The use of Birches is not generally recommended, since they are short lived trees which are at present suffering from various forms of fungus disease and insect pests which make them difficult to manage. An occasional white birch, planted against a group of evergreens, is effective, but their use should be discouraged in large quantities.*

The other trees considered undesireable for planting at Princeton were:

Ashes (*Fraxinus americana*)
Honey Locust (*Gleditschia triacanthus*)
Kentucky Coffee Tree (*Gymnocladus canadensis*)
Black Walnut (*Juglans nigra*)
all poplars (*Populus nigra, monolifera,* etc.)
Pin Oak (*Quercus palestris*)
Gingko (*Salisburia adiantifolia*)
Locust (*Robinia pseudacacie*)

The trees Farrand found most suited to general use on the campus were:

Sugar Maple (*Acer saccharum*)
Horsechestnut (*Aesculus hippocastanum*)
Catalpa (*Catalpa bignonioides*)
Beech, both American and European (*Fagus ferruginea* and *sylvatica*)
Sweet Gum (*Liquidambar styraciflua*)
Cucumber Tree (*Magnolia acuminata*)
American Buttonwood (*Platanus occidentalis*)
White Oak (*Quercus alba*) and the Swamp White Oak (*Quercus* bicolor)
Sassafras (*Sassafras officinalis*)
two or three varieties of the Linden: the Basswood (*Tilia americana*), the European variety (*Tilia europae*a)
American Elm (*Ulmus americana*)
Tulip (*Liriodendron tulipifera*)—"the best tree for general use"

These lists and the principles laid out in Farrand's initial reports guided the planting of the Graduate College, which by the 1920s had most of its planting installed in two quadrangles, Old (fig. 85) and New (fig. 78), and the Dean of the Graduate College's garden at Wyman House. These three units and their general setting remain today as places where the essence of Farrand's landscaping can still be felt.

In 1928, Farrand finally was able to hire a true plantsperson who could propagate plants from seed and grow them to full size in the nursery. She hired James Clark, a Scotsman who had been in the States for only one year. He had worked on large estates in Scotland, the last being Crathes Castle outside of Aberdeen (now a Scottish National Trust property). Clark came to America to work at Greystone, the Untermeier estate in Yonkers. In a 1984 conversation, Clark recalled his 1928 interview with Beatrix Farrand: "I went to her office in New York—She had three or four women working for her there—and she described the job and where it was. I went down to look at the place to make sure it was not a desert, and once I saw it had a good array of plants, I took it and worked at it all my life." Clark retired as Princeton's Director of Buildings and Grounds in 1962, some years after

85. Two cedars from the Cilician Mountains given by Charles Sprague Sargent to Dean West and planted in the Old Quad, the Graduate College, Princeton University. Photograph: Alan Ward.

Beatrix Farrand had ceased to work for the university. "The magnolia on the southwest corner of Pyne, that was the very first tree I planted there. There weren't magnolias on campus before that one. That magnolia is still there and prospering."

Farrand and Clark quickly developed a method for working during her campus visits that never varied during the following years. Whether she came six or two times a year, the procedure remained the same. On Friday afternoons, in the apartment she always reserved at the Princeton Inn, they reviewed the work outlined on Farrand's previous visit. On Saturday, they toured the whole campus. Farrand spent Sunday at the inn, sketching, writing about new items needing attention, changing a design or creating a new one, writing notes for her next memo. On Monday, until her afternoon departure, she and Clark reviewed their ideas at each site and gathered material for the memo outlining work to be done before their next session. Clark then had the memo typed from their notes. After reviewing every item, he would send a copy to Farrand. "Sometimes I changed some of the things she told me to do. 'Beautiful Mr. Clark, just beautiful,' she would say if she liked it." Of their fifteen years of joint work, he says, "we got on very harmoniously."

Behind every good landscape is a good gardener. In campus landscaping, the head gardener is particularly crucial to the realization of the design. Without his skill and sympathy there is no landscape. So part of the story of the Princeton campus landscape is James Clark's (fig. 86). The photograph shows him during his active years. Now ninety-three, he still lives in Princeton. Gardeners and landscapers have the reputation of being long-lived. Farrand lived to the age of eighty-seven.

Clark's house is surrounded by specimens of plants he propagated at the nursery. *Hydrangea petiolaris* and *Hydrangea saxifraga,* used at the university, climb his walls. Asked where he had obtained the latter, since commercial nurseries never seem to carry it, Clark said it had been propagated by

86. James Clark, former Head Gardener, Princeton University. Courtesy of James Clark.

seed at the Princeton nursery; it was not available commercially. Farrand's point about having a nursery has been borne out here.

Clark was responsible for putting in and maintaining Princeton's wall plantings. Farrand described his duties thus: "Mr. Clark was given the distinctly horticultural problems of the campus landscape gardening. It is he who trains the wall plants, prunes the shrubs, and starts whatever little plants can be grown without the aid of the small propagating house which is so sorely needed"[47] Many of the special trees around the campus and its vicinity were propagated from seed by him at the university nursery. "Three or four cold frames is all I had for propagating when I started. Then about ten years later [actually 1935, seven years later] we got a forty-foot greenhouse which made things much better."

Today, the old nursery is weedy and overgrown. In its heyday, it covered six acres, "and I had it full to overflowing," Clark says. He thinks he had at least five thousand plants there, used ultimately throughout the campus. The memos show it was the heart of the landscaping operation. A smaller nursery has today replaced the original.

One of the planting memos written during the long collaboration between Farrand and Clark reveals the harmoniousness and professionalism of their relationship. Dated 12 July 1933, it clearly indicates their joint authorship and the concerns that occupied each of them.

> *When it proves necessary an additional sum of $30. or $40 may be spent for* Kalmia latifolia *needed for the extension of the plantation at Prospect. Mr. Macmillan should be asked whether this may be taken from the Prospect fund or if it is necessary to charge it to our small Tree Fund. . . .*
>
> *Mrs. Farrand is trying to get some* Narcissus biflorus *which is a two flowered narcissus, as its name implies, and which spreads rapidly from the original cultivated stock in Virginia. This would be attractive to use in naturalizing positions where a good strong growing sort is needed. It might be well to cultivate this narcissus for a few years in the nursery until the stock is obtained. . . .*
>
> *The plan for planting the Graduate College north quadrangle has been sent to Mrs. Ruth Walters, who is glad to have it and writes that she will be willing to send further funds for plants when these are needed. . . .*

Possibly it might be well to purchase $15, or $20, worth of daffodils for growing in the nursery. . . .

The question is raised as to whether it is wise to buy two tons of Rhody-Life from Wilson when possible, or whether it might be well to experiment with the acid fertilizer which is used with mosses at Yale, consisting of 1 part Nitrate of Soda, 2 parts Superphosphate, and 1 part Nitrate of Potash. This is sold by the American Agricultural Chemical Company at so much the hundred pounds. Possibly a special rate could be obtained for the University. . . .

Mr. Macmillan is to be asked whether there may be a possibility of getting the surplus white pine from the Yale University Nursery. . . .

When it is possible to purchase some seats to use near McCosh and the other dormitories this should be done. The teak seats cost approximately $50, delivered at Princeton. Will Mr. Macmillan kindly keep this in mind as the purchase of a seat or two each year will not add much to the upkeep costs and the benches are found to give great pleasure to the students at other colleges. . . .

It was decided to make a nursery for Ericaceae on the south side of the present one and Mrs. Farrand said she would try to collect material for this as well as to get seed for Mr. Clark for his own raising. Mr. Benjamin Y. Morrison of the Bureau of Plant Industry of the Department of Agriculture at Washington said he would gladly cooperate in adding to the nursery's ericaceous material when this becomes available. . . .

As the three eastern Colleges with which Mrs. Farrand is associated are all willing to share their surplus nursery stock it is suggested that when the censuses are taken a copy be written which may be passed around from one instituton to the other so that the surplus may be available for the other university nurseries provided the cost of its digging and packing and the transportation be paid for. The University at Yale has contributed some magnolias to the University of Chicago and the University of Chicago hopes later to be able to reciprocate by giving Yale some of its surplus roses. This sort of exchange is often a benefit to both universities.

Today, only about fifty percent of Farrand's Princeton landscaping is still visible, but it covers a sizable portion of the campus—in fragments and whole pieces—and achieves some bold effects. Still setting the distinctive tone of the campus, it is in other respects like a painting kept in a closet. It waits to be discovered.

Yale University (1922–1945)

By far, Yale is the most interesting of the other campuses Farrand designed that approximated Princeton's scope. Here she also was asked to design a major new Gothic complex, the Harkness Quadrangle. The quadrangle closely resembled Princeton's Graduate College in aim and style. If Cram had been alive, he would have designed it. Instead, it was the work of James Gamble Rogers. Today it consists of three residential colleges that surround inner courtyards: Branford (fig. 87), Saybrook, and Jonathan Edwards. Only Branford and Silliman College (a separate and later commission not a part of the Harkness Quadrangle) retain any aspect of Farrand's original interior courtyards in recognizable shape. In addition, the exteriors of these residential colleges that face city streets—Yale sits in the heart of urban New Haven—have one very successful feature attributed to Farrand: tree-planted moats. A waist-high wall separates the sidewalk traffic from the lower ground beside the college; windows allow light into its basement level. Farrand planted native trees here. The dogwoods, witchhazels, hawthorns, and viburnums bloom in the spring or change color in the fall, making the streets more interesting than most sidewalk trees do (pl. XIII).

Farrand began her Yale commission on 1 January 1923, though she had already been at work at Yale for several months, on a visiting basis. A letter from Yale, dated 12 October 1922, asks Farrand to landscape the Sterling Laboratory as well as the quadrangle. And a letter dated 30 October acknowledges her acceptance of the position as Yale's Consulting Landscape Gardener, to begin on 1 January 1923. Comptroller Thomas Farnam cited the need for such a person after Farrand had begun work on the Harkness Quadrangle. He noted that all other landscape operations had been haphazard and unplanned. Once she had accepted this commission, Farrand re-

87. Yew hedge planted in one of the Branford College courtyards, Yale University. Photograph: Alan Ward.

ceived a fixed salary, rather than payment by the visit.

With the Princeton experience behind her, Farrand first worked to hire knowledgeable plantpersons. George Cromie, also the City Forester, became responsible for the Harkness Quadrangle; George C. Murray took charge of the Yale Botanic Garden and future nursery. By February 1923, the staff was in place.

Next in importance was a nursery. In a letter to the university dated November 1922, Farrand says it is "essential . . . there be a nursery started . . . [because] buying oversized material is expensive." Even prior to her appointment, she had submitted a detailed proposal for the nursery. Her Princeton work had familiarized her with the cost of different operations, and as I mentioned earlier, she suggested an accounting method based on this experience. The nursery began operating in the fall of 1923. On 15 April 1925, Farrand mentioned that the thousand plants George Murray had grown from seed at the Botanical Garden and nursery were ready for spring planting.[48]

Because the nursery was established early and in completed form, we know what it cost. Conditioning the two acres for planting, and stocking and maintaining it, cost $5,000 a year (the equivalent of $27,500 in 1983). Since any large, well-grown specimen tree today can cost about $5,000, this budget is hardly large. Yet this kind of work had never been done on university campuses before. Landscaping had not even been considered a design issue until the late nineteenth century.

By the time Farrand began her work at Yale, others were doing related pioneering work there, particularly in the Forestry School. And it was at Yale that Professor George Marsh of the Forestry School had written one of the first and most influential books on ecology, *Man and Nature* (1864). Yale was a place where Farrand's ideas could flourish.

The Yale nursery was started in 1923 with fifteen-hundred plants. The immediate aims were to:

1. Propagate wild flowers
2. Experiment with forest tree seedlings, experiments to be conducted by Professor Toumey
3. Propagate shrubs and small trees in greenhouse to free Univer-

sity of commercial nurseries; the Arnold Arboretum to cooperate by sending cuttings, seeds and plants

4. Build up an arboretum
5. Secure additional grounds for the nursery[49]

To launch the nursery, Farrand had enlisted the help of her mentor at the Arnold Arboretum. "My old friend and teacher, . . . Sargent, said that the Arboretum would cooperate in every possible way with schemes we had in mind."[50] He sent her plants.[51]

At Yale, Farrand was able to connect the nursery with a botanical garden, for which money had been donated by Professor Othniel C. Marsh of the Botany Department. She suggested that the new botanical garden be based on the one in Padua, built in the manner of a walled, medieval garden. The Padua garden had associations for Farrand. Edith Wharton, her aunt, had singled it out for praise in her 1904 book, *Italian Villas and their Gardens*. There is a Farrand design in the Yale University folder in the Farrand Collection at Berkeley for a botanical garden related in style to that of Padua. However a later design of hers, with an informal character, seems to have been adopted. The Berkeley collection also includes the plan for the later garden and the design for the buildings and the entrance to the whole complex (fig. 97).

Responding to Farrand's request, a Yale official described the relationship between Yale's botanical garden, established first, and the nursery which followed at its heels:

> *I understand a nursery will be started, and that this will be under the direction of and will be operated by the Botanical Garden. That it is intended to raise at first only the more expensive type of plants. The propagating of the small plants would be done at the Botanical Garden itself; that the plants would then be moved to a nursery to develop, and I understand also that certain types of specimens might be planted about the grounds where they would serve a decorative purpose for a time, and either by thinning or removal would be transplanted later to permanent locations. Such planting about the grounds I suppose would automatically remove these plants from the care of the Botanical Garden.*[52]

To university officials, Farrand pointed out the great number of plants provided by the nursery at a fraction of the cost of commercial purchases. "Mr. Murray has already grown . . . over 1000 plants which may be used in the University's planting this spring."[53] She also mentioned the relatively modest cost of running the nursery.

In the course of propagating seeds from different sources, Farrand conducted an interesting experiment for the grounds of the Sterling School of Medicine. It was very much in keeping with the Arts & Crafts principle of using plants as symbols. On 26 May 1924, she reported that "through the kindness of Mrs. J. Pierpont Morgan [for whom she was also designing at the time] we hope to have some day the descendants of the plane tree under which Hippocrates taught in the island of Kos growing on the grounds of the Sterling Medical School. Mrs. Morgan collected the seed and knowing how deeply interested I am in the work at Yale has sent me a few of the buttons from the old tree."[54]

At Yale, as at Princeton, Farrand had her share of professional conflicts. Architect James Gamble Rogers wrote in 1931:

> *You will perhaps say (and with some reason) that inasmuch as I am no longer Advisor to the Plan Committee, my opinion is not wanted in regard to the planting, but when one has studied a building really in relation to the planting, he naturally has a desire that the planting will be done to bring out the best points as studied on the sketches and plans. For that reason, I cannot help but tell you how disappointed I was in the planting in Davenport and Pierson. I will mention only a few things:*
>
> *In Pierson, the plan of the court was made irregular in order to take advantage of every inch of our property and make the court appear as large as possible. To overcome this irregularity, we counted always on having the trees frame the symmetry at each end with a tree framed vista between the trees thus counteracting the effect of the irregularity and giving an appearance of spaciousness.*
>
> *As now planted, this vista effect which is the most important thing about the plan, has not only not been carried out but in addition, there has been planted near the middle of the court a large, very thick, bushy, low*

growing tree that besides greatly cutting down the apparent size of the court blocks up the two important vistas so necessary to the best effect.

At each door is put two evergreens (as I remember, yews) that give a very flippant effect to the othewise dignity of the colonial architecture and gives an effect of a suburban milliner's cemetery. I have never seen in the colonial any such planting which is only a development of the last thirty years for suburban homes.

The same effect was used in the Memorial Quadrangle against my wishes and I think has been the discordant note in that group though in a Gothic building it does not give the extremely unpleasant air it does in the Colonial.

Others at Yale looked with greater favor on her work. In New Haven, as at Princeton, Farrand designed and maintained the private gardens of certain university officials. One belonged to Yale's president (fig. 88), the other to Comptroller Thomas Farnam (for the comptroller's garden, we have no surviving plan). In January of 1925, Farnam told Farrand, "I have enjoyed my garden more than ever this year and though perhaps it is a luxury I have reached the stage where I consider it absolutely necessary to my comfort and welfare."[55]

The Depression affected Farrand's landscaping at Yale by causing major budget cuts and staff reductions (from sixty to forty).[56] George Cromie suggested that the university ask students to help with landscaping and offer scholarships for doing so. During the Depression years, Farrand purchased no plants for the campus, but used trees and bushes produced by the nursery exclusively.[57]

The data on Farrand's work at Yale shows that she landscaped many parts of the campus and had a major impact. The list below identifies the buildings that she landscaped.

Sterling Chemistry Laboratory
Lapham Field House
Sterling Hall of Medicine
Botanical Garden and Nursery

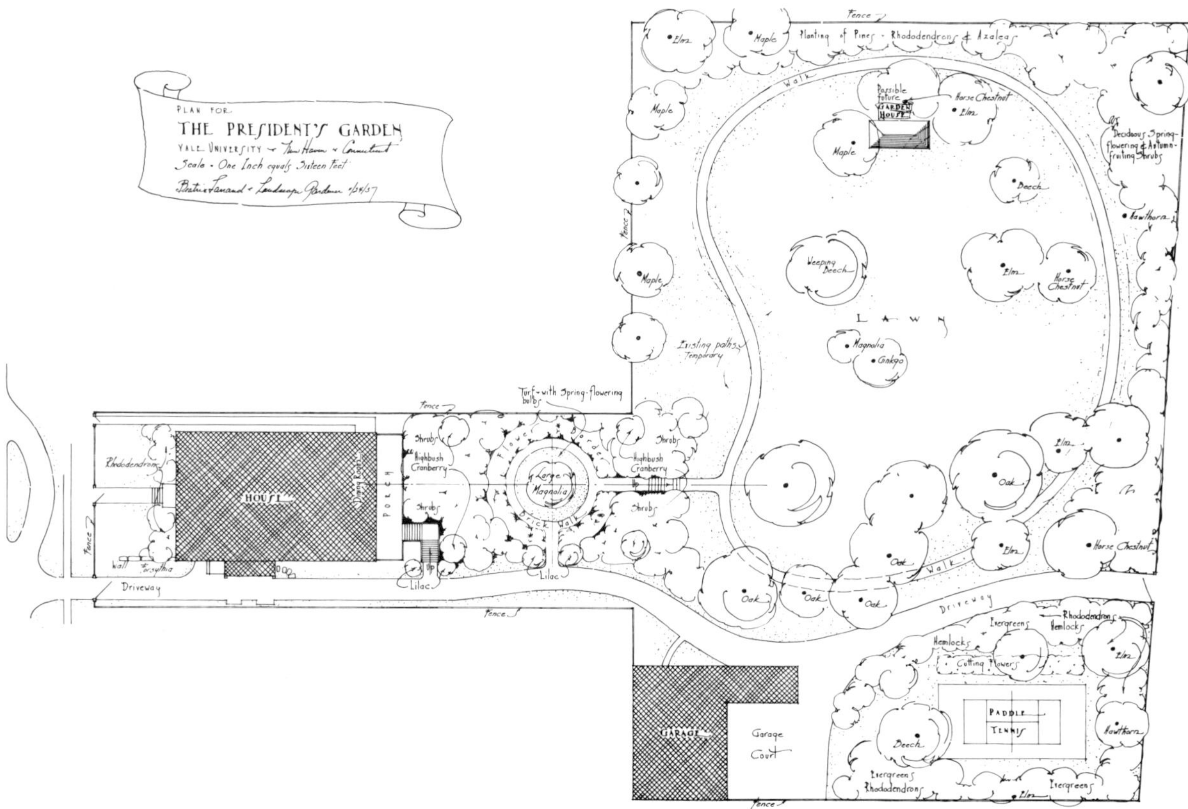

88. Plan of the President's garden, Yale University. Courtesy of University of California, Berkeley; Department of Landscape Architecture; Documents Collection.

Harkness Quadrangle (now Branford, Jonathan Edwards, and Saybrook colleges)
Peabody Museum
Sheffield Hall (front)
Nathan Smith Hall
Weir Hall
Sage Hall
Sloane
President's House
Berkeley Oval
Yale Divinity School
New Haven Hospital
Silliman College

Figure 89, a 1980s map, shows the landscaped areas that still exist. Unfortunately, when Yale had to expand within the city after World War II, much of her work was lost, particularly at the hospital/medical and science sections, but also on portions of the main campus. As mentioned earlier, extant pieces include the Branford College courtyards in Harkness Quadrangle as well as Silliman College and the moats surrounding both colleges. Other areas have lost many of their plantings or their basic layouts have been changed. The nursery is gone, though small pieces of the Botanical Garden remain. Amidst its overgrown trees, the remnants of its old rock garden can still be seen, resembling isolated archaeological remains.

OTHER CAMPUSES

In respect to other campuses, only what is unique to each will be mentioned here. It should be kept in mind, however, that in each case Farrand's general principles were applied. Nurseries were proposed for every campus.

The University of Chicago (1929–1936)

At Chicago, Farrand was asked to landscape a campus where a master plan of 1891 had adopted a quadrangular layout and, again, the Gothic style which would allow for variety within a unified whole. But there was more to the choice than that.

> *The choice of Gothic for the University over the popular classicism of the [World's] Columbian Exposition [being built simultaneously in Chicago] had its sources in the University's conception of itself. Classic buildings were financed by merchant princes, Gothic buildings arose through the combined efforts of humble workmen. Classicism referred to Europe's palaces, Gothic to Europe's great seats of learning. Classicism stood for the burgeoning materialism of the Renaissance, Gothic for timeless religious values.*[58]

Farrand came to work on a campus conceived completely in the Gothic spirit. By the time she had finished her work at Chicago in 1936, the Collegiate-Gothic style was going out of fashion.

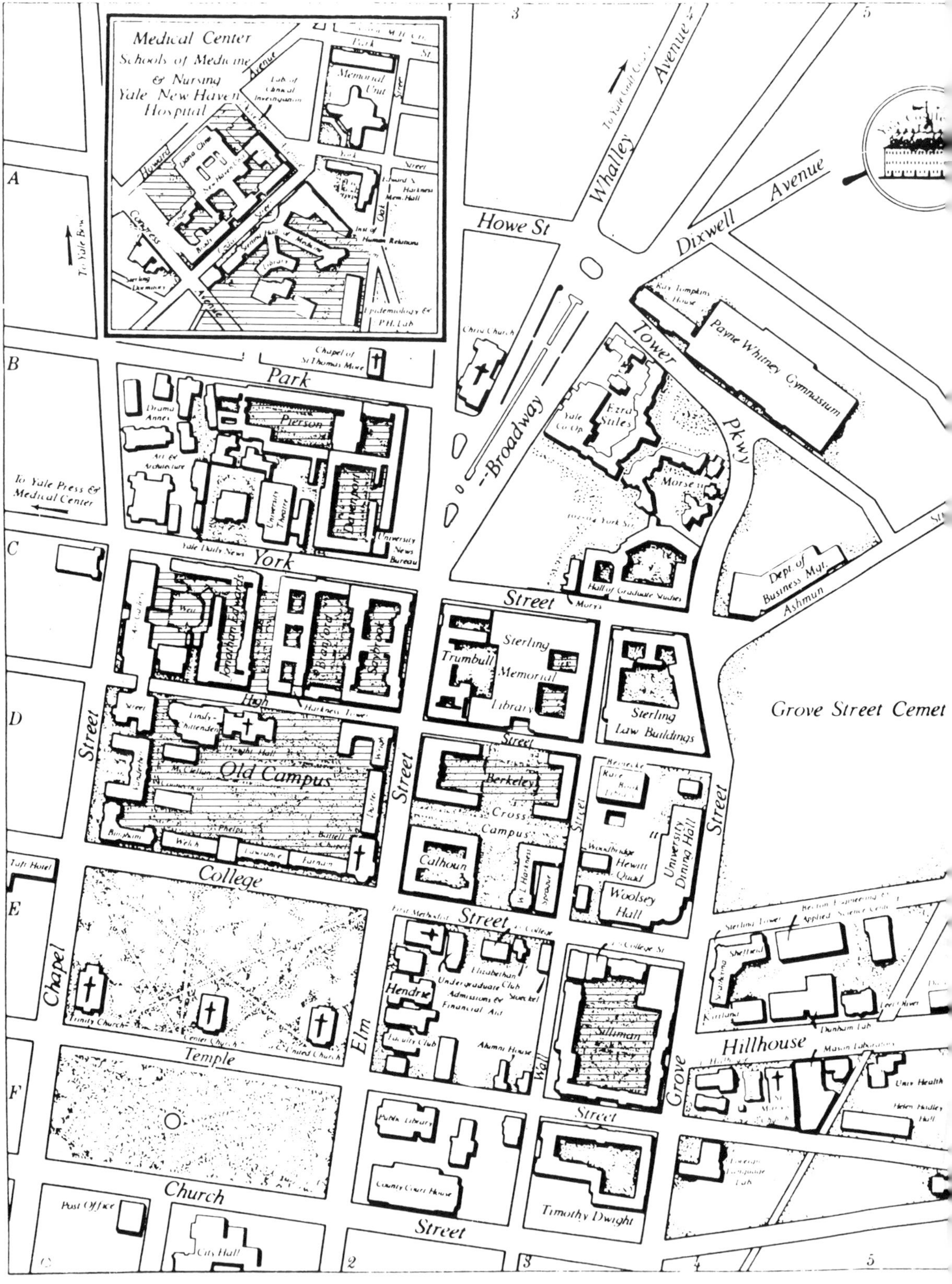

Medical Center
Schools of Medicine & Nursing
Yale New Haven Hospital
Memorial Unit
Edward S. Harkness Mem. Hall
Sterling Hall of Medicine
Library
Sterling Dormitory
Epidemiology & P.H. Lab
Congress Avenue
Howard
York Street
Park
To Yale Bowl
To Yale Press & Medical Center
Chapel of St. Thomas More
Christ Church
Howe St
Whalley Avenue
To Yale Golf Course
Dixwell Avenue
Ray Tompkins House
Payne Whitney Gymnasium
Tower Pkwy
Broadway
Yale Co-Op
Ezra Stiles
Morse
Hall of Graduate Studies
Mory's
Dept. of Business Mgt.
Ashmun
Drama Annex
Art & Architecture
Pierson
University Theatre
Davenport
University News Bureau
Yale Daily News
York
Street
Jonathan Edwards
Branford
Saybrook
Trumbull
Sterling Memorial Library
Sterling Law Buildings
Grove Street Cemet
High
Harkness Tower
Street
Linsly-Chittenden
Dwight Hall
Old Campus
Phelps
Welch
Battell Chapel
Farnam
Berkeley
Cross Campus
Calhoun
Beinecke Rare Book Library
Woodbridge
Hewitt Quad
University Dining Hall
Woolsey Hall
Street
Taft Hotel
College
Street
Chapel
Trinity Church
Center Church
United Church
Temple
Elm
First Methodist
Hendrie
Elizabethan Club
Undergraduate Admissions & Financial Aid
Faculty Club
Alumni House
Wall
Silliman
College St
Sterling Tower
Becton Engineering & Applied Science Center
Sheffield
Kirtland
Dunham Lab
Hillhouse
Mason Laboratory
Grove
St. Mary's Church
Univ. Health
Helen Hadley Hall
Street
Public Library
County Court House
Timothy Dwight
Church
Street
Post Office
City Hall
A
B
C
D
E
F
3
5
2
3
5

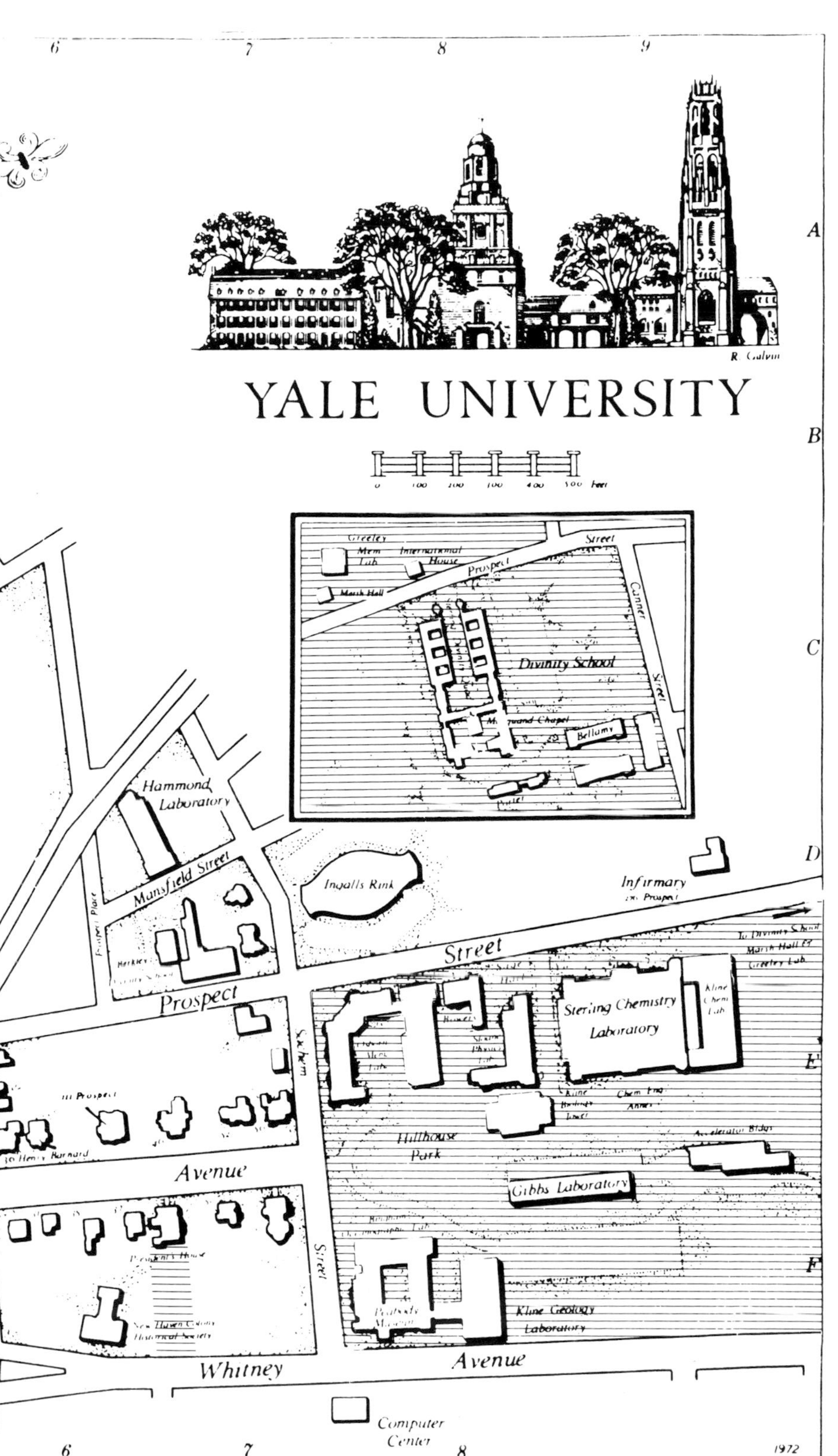

89. Map of Yale University in the 1980s; areas landscaped by Farrand are crosshatched.

The University of Chicago hired Farrand in 1929. After having consulted different landscape firms through its early years, the university wanted to secure a general landscape plan.

> *For seventeen years she has been the consultant for Princeton on all their planning and has been the adviser on planting in connection with the Harkness group at Yale, and all work since then. . . . It appears that Mrs. Farrand from the standpoint of a long experience with direct relation to campus requirements is especially well fitted for our needs and it is recommended that the Business Manager be authorized to engage Mrs. Farrand in the capacity of consulting landscape gardener.*[59]

Farrand's fee from the university was $75.00 per day.

Farrand emphasized to Chicago the importance of direct supervision of the actual work on the first plantings; later work would require less supervision because those in charge of campus gardening would have the experience to handle it. A head gardener topped her list of priorities.

The onset of the Depression restricted the dimensions of Farrand's work at Chicago. Her major change of the central quadrangle's roads and walks, though approved, was never implemented. And though she made plans for the university buildings listed below, these were often adjustments rather than full designs. The following buildings received her attention:

Oriental Institute
International House
Bobs Roberts Hospital
Eckhart Hall
Botany Greenhouses and Laboratory
Blaine Hall
Men's Residence Halls
Hicks McElwee
Jones Laboratory
Women's Quadrangle
Ida Noyes Hall block
Yerkes Observatory

Kent Laboratory
Hitchcock Court
Cobb Hall
Hutchinson Court

Full plans do exist for the International House's courtyard.

Farrand also began designing for the Sunny Gymnasium (where the Yale forsythia was planted). And she started a nursery, obtaining stock from the Morton Arboretum. A list of the original plants survives, consisting mainly of trees that were native to or could be naturalized in the area:

Shadblows: *Amelanchier laevis*
Amelanchier oblongifolia

Crabapples: *Malus coronaria*
Malus floribunda
Malus ioensis
Malus ioensis bechteli

Syringa japonica
Viburnum lentago

Magnolias

The nursery was to be large enough to grow fifteen-hundred shrubs and trees and four to five thousand ground covers. She suggested that the University of Chicago contact Yale and Princeton about the costs of running the nursery.[60]

In her work at Chicago, Farrand made one interesting addition to her working method, relating to the planting of vines on buildings. When asked how high the vines should be trained to grow, she answered that "each building is an individual problem," suggesting the use of a separate card for each that would show the ultimate effect desired and the height of trained vines. "These cards can be used by each gardener at each building to assure steady progress towards our ultimate aim."[61] In her wall plantings at Chicago she experimented with crabapples espaliered along the walls in a palmette form.

Oberlin College (1939–1946)

> *Mr. Lester S. Ries, Superintendent of Buildings and Grounds for Oberlin College, and formerly Assistant Superintendent of Buildings and Grounds for the University of Chicago, has told us of your interesting and beautiful work for the University of Chicago and for other educational institutions. We are now in need of advice and consulting service on the planting and care of our campus and grounds, particularly with relation to the prospective construction of a Memorial Auditorium, but also with attention to the modification of present planting so as to develop an harmonious plan for all of the College grounds.*[62]

On 3 October 1939, Oberlin hired Farrand as a consultant. Her fee here was $100.00 per day (equivalent to $700.00 in 1983) plus travel expenses and the separate charges for office work.

The Oberlin commission differed from others. The village of Oberlin and the college were very much intertwined, so Farrand planned to landscape Tappan Square, which doubled as the village and the campus green, as an area that took something from both the campus's and the town's character. She went about the overall scheme for Oberlin with her usual speed:

> *It is suggested that instead of a preliminary journey and view of the problems, we go straight to work, as it may be possible to formulate some sort of a scheme in a day or two on which the college can work for a considerable time to come, without further visits from me. If this idea appeals to you as sensible, a letter will be sent you regarding my terms and the method in which I work, if indeed this has not already been dispatched to you earlier.*[63]

In accordance with her general principle regarding the use of native plants, she here suggested the planting of "crabs and haws."

Though Farrand's appointment in 1939 as Consulting Landscape Architect to Oberlin College was indefinite, her work ended in 1946 when a new president took office.

Hamilton College (1920s)

Regarding Farrand's work at Hamilton, no documentation has survived at the college. The Farrand Collection at Berkeley contains the site survey for the central quadrangle and the landscape plans for a few faculty houses, as well as planting lists for many academic buildings (the Science Building being the landscape she was hired initially to do). The list of buildings on which she worked is extensive and indicates that she was indeed responsible for most of the campus landscaping, certainly for all the buildings on the central quadrangle.[64] An anecdote told by Professor Willard Thorpe of Princeton, who was a student at Hamilton in the 1920s, describes Farrand walking the central quadrangle with stakes in her hand, accompanied by the president and treasurer of the college, supposedly marking the placement of trees. The surviving list of trees for planting the campus shows us again a stress on native plants. Farrand specified that the Carnegie Building would be planted entirely with different species of *Berberis* and the Hall of Science with different species of viburnums. One of the surviving landscape plans for a faculty house shows a planting with different species of crabapples.

Farrand was reported to have had the vegetation cut on the edge of the hill on which Hamilton stands so that the valley below could be viewed from the central quadrangle[65] (advice worth repeating to Hamilton College today, for that view has been lost again to encroaching vegetation). This was very much in keeping with ideas in Charles Sargent's Boston landscape circle (as can be seen in the illustrations in Charles Eliot's book, *Charles Eliot, Landscape Architect,* Boston, 1902, where views are opened up in tree-clogged valleys).

Vassar College (1926–1927)

Landscape plans for Main's forecourt (fig. 90) and a few other buildings, such as Kendrick, have survived at Berkeley, but no written material on Farrand's involvement with the campus seems to have survived at Vassar. The plans show exterior boundaries of evergreens around service courts and mass planting of viburnums, laurels, and azaleas (around Kendrick, for example).

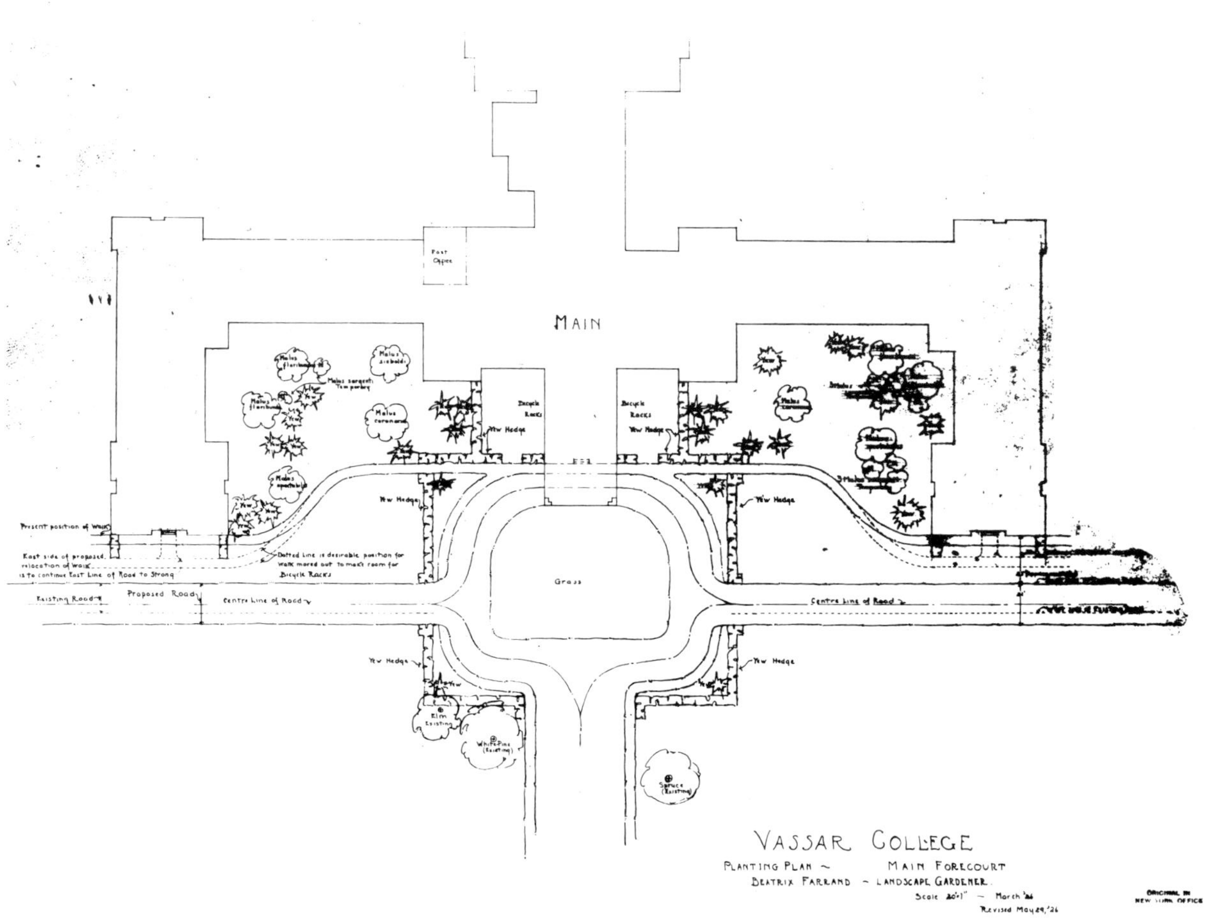

90. Landscape plan for the Main forecourt, Vassar College. Courtesy of University of California, Berkeley; Department of Landscape Architecture; Documents Collection.

California Campuses

Farrand was involved in the landscaping of two educational institutions in California, the California Institute of Technology at Pasadena (1928–1938) and Occidental College in Los Angeles (1937–1940), but the data is scant on the amount of her work there. We know she designed the entrance courtyard at the latter (fig. 91) and the Dabney courtyard at the first. Here, as in most of her California work, she was associated with California architect

Myron Hunt. Her quadrangle at Occidental College, though worse for wear, is still intact except for the loss of a few large eucalyptus in front.

Dabney Court, the only intact piece of Farrand's landscaping at the California Institute of Technology, is a gem set in the rest of the institute landscape. A planting of olive trees and grass, with some low plants at the edges of the courtyard, seems so simple as not to be much of a planting at all. But it is a very subtle piece of design, with low walls all around it creating a cloistered, peaceful space different from any other on the campus. The openings on the campus were studied carefully and lined up with particular views.

> *Move the present gateway in the east wall of [the] garden further to the north so that it will be directly opposite the gateway into Dabney Garden. Move one or two of the small flowering eucalyptus trees so that when they grow larger they will balance the olive trees in the Dabney Garden opposite.*[66]

The olive trees are not just any olive trees. They have been shaped for maximum effect and have grown into sculptures with silver leaves—the shaping and pruning done under Farrand's direct supervision.[67] Here the effect of peace and serenity stands out on a campus landscaped mainly by others, and here it can be more readily observed than on those campuses where she imparted that atmosphere to the whole. It is interesting that she created a walled courtyard here in a campus that was otherwise on an open plan.

Farrand produced a careful report for the landscaping of the western portion of the campus, on which she worked in fits and starts from 1932 to 1938 but with no real appreciation of her professional services (as seen in the correspondence quoted earlier). The correspondence reveals that Farrand encountered difficulties with each service rendered. Clearly, her general design was never fully carried out.

In spite of the difficulties in implementation and the lack of interest in landscaping at the institute, true to her beliefs even here, Farrand proposed a modest nursery. She suggested "that a small nursery of trees be established at the Biology Farm in Arcadia and that fifty young trees be pur-

91. The central quadrangle of Occidental College in the 1930s. Courtesy of University of California, Berkeley; Department of Landscape Architecture; Documents Collection.

chased for development in this nursery, namely: thirty oaks, ten native palms, and ten olive trees." The cost of these trees about three feet high would be approximately one hundred dollars.[68]

The Pennsylvania School of Horticulture for Women (1932)

A general plan by Beatrix Farrand exists for the gardens of the Pennsylvania School of Horticulture for Women, with a detailed design for two arbors with a fountain at one end of the garden. The existing garden's design, however, has been credited to Albert Bush Brown. The Pennsylvania School now belongs to Temple University. No correspondence regarding the garden survives,[69] but recent photographs indicate that the overall layout of the garden follows that of Farrand's 1932 plan and the arbors are like those she designed. Clearly, we must credit Farrand at least in part with the design of this garden. In time it may be possible to sort out the contributions of each of these noted landscape architects.

OTHER PUBLIC INSTITUTIONS

Most studies of Farrand reveal her as a traditional, European-type landscaper, working on the private gardens of the wealthy. Marlene Salon's pioneering work[70] gave us the first glimpse of that side of Farrand's practice. Only gradually are we beginning to capture another area—her work in the public realm. The first attention to this aspect was in Richard Lyon's paper on her campuses.[71] As I have tried to demonstrate here, we must now regard these campuses as a major component of her professional activity. But, Farrand did other work in the public realm as well. She designed a garden for the White House. Three astronomical observatories bear evidence of her attention, and—perhaps not surprisingly—she produced designs for two city-run botanic gardens. Moreover two of her most important private gardens came ultimately to be associated with public institutions, and she involved herself deeply in their transition from private to public use.

Observatories

Four astronomical observatories stand out as distinct pieces of Farrand's work. In two cases they were related to her work for universities—Princeton and Chicago—but they were treated as separate and special designs. A third (fig. 92) was for George E. Hale, a California Institute of Technology astronomer who had his living quarters and a solar observatory built as one with private and foundation money. Farrand also appears to have done some

92. Study for gardens at the George E. Hale Observatory, Pasadena. Courtesy of University of California, Berkeley; Department of Landscape Architecture; Documents Collection.

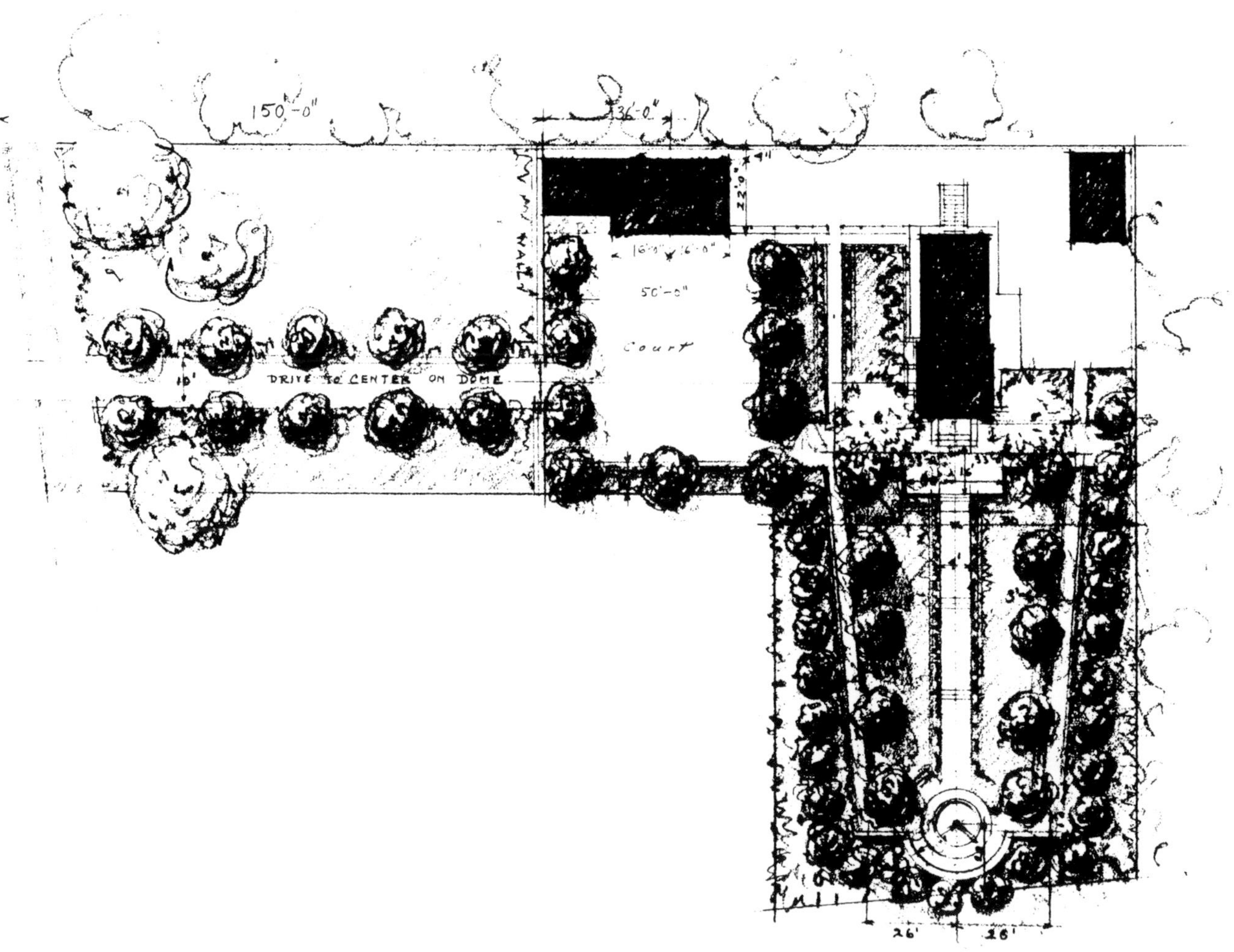

work for the California Institute of Technology on the site of its Mount Palomar Observatory.

In the late nineteenth century, observatories were charged with special meaning and were sited very carefully, as Paul Venable Turner has pointed out in a recent book on the development of the American college and university campus.

> *In the 1830s, a new type of bulding appeared at the American college that allowed an even grander and more sublime view of nature: the astronomical observatory. . . . The fashion spread swiftly throughout the country. . . . Motives were the attraction of nature itself and a burgeoning student interest in the neglected area of science. . . . Often it was set well apart . . . to allow the professor and his students to observe the universe in an inspiring scene of unspoiled nature.*[72]

The George E. Hale Solar Observatory (1928) still stands nearly intact, though its vegetation is overgrown. A part of its land was sold, but a section with cypresses planted by Farrand can still be seen. The observatory itself has been more recently sold to a private purchaser who intends to restore and preserve this unique building. The plan of the landscape here is particularly interesting, with a long approach centered on the dome. There is a square parking lot fronting the observatory that is surrounded by a tall hedge of *Myrtus communis* which hides the cars from view and serves as a dark "wall" behind which the observatory rises. Surrounded by bas reliefs of the sun and high, dark vegetation, the observatory still seems imbued with the magic that astronomy held for this era.

The White House Garden (1913–1916)

There was a White House garden designed by Farrand while Woodrow Wilson was president. Whether it was Wilson's Princeton connection that brought her to the White House we do not know, but it seems most likely. There are a few extant drawings (pl. XIV) to give an idea of the plan, but no correspondence reveals what was asked for and no photographs show it after completion.

City Botanic Gardens

The Santa Barbara Botanic Garden (1938–1959) is one of the most beautiful in the United States, partly because of its site and natural vegetation and partly because of the overall plan, which heightened and intensified certain of these natural qualities. Both Farrand and Lockwood De Forest, a very talented Santa Barbara landscape architect, worked on this project. The Santa Barbara project must have been personally difficult because Farrand was seen as an interloper in California and the local professionals never had much use for her.

This situation plagued Farrand's California work, but she could do little about it. She spent only a few months of every year in the state since she never could get enough California commissions to maintain a full Los Angeles office. Her involvement with the botanic garden came through the Bliss family of Dumbarton Oaks. Mildred Bliss's mother, Anna Blakesley Bliss, endowed the botanic garden. (Farrand also landscaped the Casa Dorinda, a house for Anna Blakesley Bliss in Santa Barbara. In both projects, she used native plants.) At the botanic garden, Farrand intervened in the original landscape only where necessary—less here than in any other of her commissions—trying to blend completely with the surrounding landscape.

Farrand served as consultant to the botanic garden from 1938 to 1959. Because De Forest was in the army by the time she wrote the main report, she had some freedom in determining the overall direction of the design. The details are full of recognizable Farrand trademarks: emphasis on the importance of steps and walks, the careful shaping of grades, and the treatment of parking lots.

Farrand's design guidelines for the garden suggest three main points, all still apparent.[73] First, "two walks centering on the boulder [a boulder with a memorial plaque] are to be emphasized, the main dramatic point of view for visitors." Second, a meadow flanked the boulder and the paths leading to it. The only open space devoid of trees, it afforded a view of one peak in the mountain range that surrounds the canyon in which the botanic garden is located (pl. XV). "Simplify its upkeep and accentuate the view of the mountains" and "eliminate the Bermuda grass meadow; replace with wild flowers if not too costly; make the wild flowers a permanent feature;

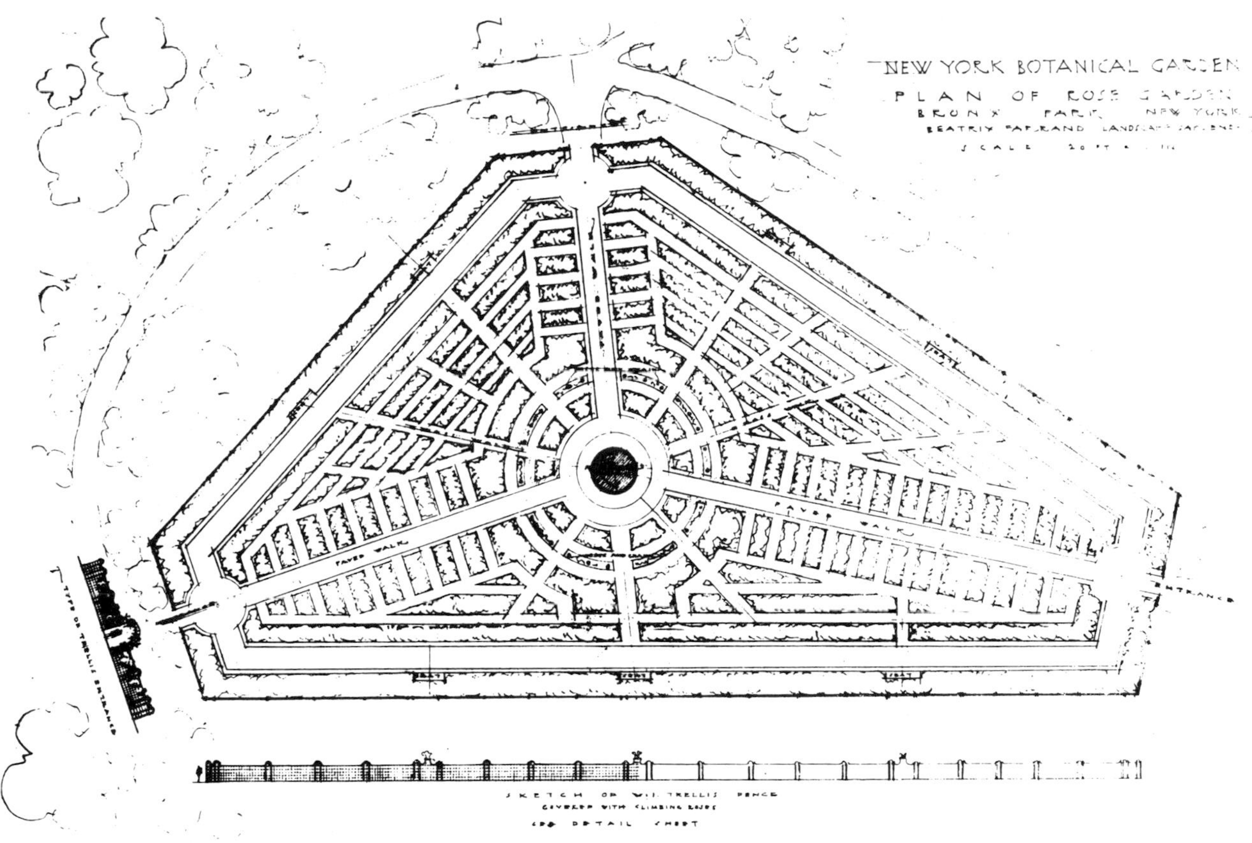

93. Plan of the Rose Garden, New York Botanical Garden, Bronx Park, with trellis detail. Courtesy of University of California, Berkeley; Department of Landscape Architecture; Documents Collection.

otherwise plant with wild strawberries." Farrand also said that the path around the meadow should be an oval, not a circle. It is an oval today. Gray foliage plants were to run northeast from the meadow up toward the hills. This planting—of the slightly grayish *Pinus coulteri* and the almost white-leaved sabias—would add perspective and give a sense of distance to this part of the meadow.

Finally, Farrand described the treatment of steps and walks mentioned earlier. Having risers of not over six inches and treads no less than twelve inches . . ."the steps should be divided into two or three runs." All the walks were to be about ten feet wide "so groups of students can walk two to three abreast," but also because the age of the automobile had begun. "Access by road-paths of truck width to reach all important centers of work will help

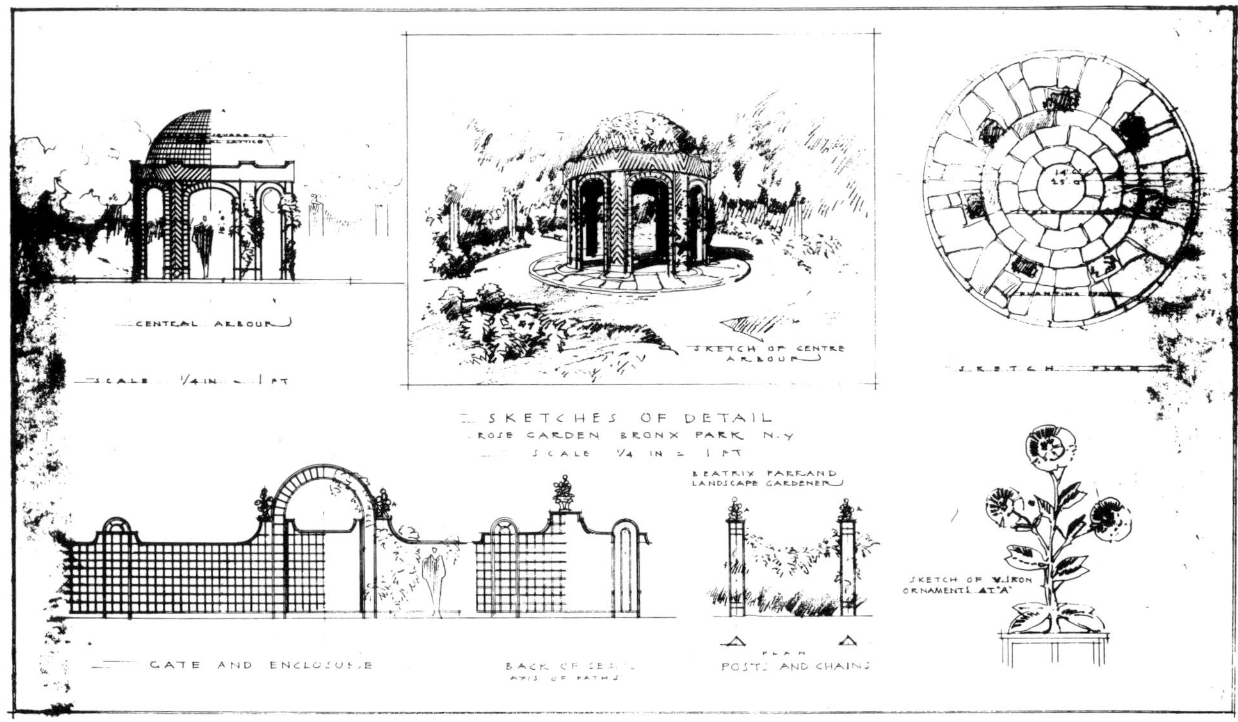

94. Sketches of details for the Rose Garden, New York Botanical Garden. Courtesy of University of California, Berkeley; Department of Landscape Architecture; Documents Collection.

keep down the cost of manual labor." In the paths, which were of earth, wheel tracks of flagstones were to be laid down for use in muddy weather. "These wide paths make it easy to plant on borders."

For the New York Botanical Garden (1915–1916), the files at Berkeley show a Farrand design for a rose garden with a beautiful floor plan and surrounding trellis (figs. 93 & 94), but no documentation accompanies the plan to fill in the voids. Yet given Farrand's later involvement and interest in botanic gardens, this early piece of work should be noted.

Dumbarton Oaks (1921–1947)

Farrand designed Dumbarton Oaks in Washington, D.C. as a private garden for the Robert Woods Blisses. The Blisses were collectors of Byzantine and Pre-Columbian art, and they encouraged scholarship in those areas as well as in garden history. After the death of Robert Bliss, their house, garden, and collections were given to Harvard University as a center for research in those fields. As the garden passed from the Blisses' hands to those of the trustees of Harvard, Mildred Bliss (who had survived her husband) suggested that Beatrix Farrand prepare a report with specific proposals as to how the Dumbarton Oaks gardens should be changed in passing from private to public use. Dumbarton Oaks, today transformed according to those specifications, represents the most perfect bridge between Farrand's two kinds of work. Though started as a private garden, we know it today as a beautiful landscape belonging to a university, and open to the general public as well as to the scholars who work in the now-converted mansion. It is thanks to this more public role that this prized piece of landscape has survived.

The proposals made for the change are tied to Farrand's campus experience, and they reiterate and reinforce the principles of campus planting that characterized her earlier work. In her report to Harvard, she stated them as general considerations ruling the garden's transformation.

First came the desire to retain the sense of remoteness from urban and street life.

> *One of the characteristics of the Dumbarton Oaks grounds is a pleasant sense of withdrawal from the nearby streets, together with the feeling of an intimate connection with all that a great city can offer. This quiet and seclusion should be preserved by care and replanting of its boundaries, and as the students will mainly be in residence during the leafless months of the year, evergreen plant material should make up the bulk of its boundary shields. For the same reason the plants immediately surrounding the house should be mainly evergreen.*

Second, she stressed the greater importance of trees in this new use of the landscape.

> *The trees, many of them of great age and beauty, should be intelligently cared for and replanting done to ensure the eventual replacement of some of the older growth. The shrubs are of somewhat secondary importance but*

nevertheless are vital to the design as a whole, so that the Forsythia hollow, the Box Ellipse, the Crabapple knoll, the Cherry slope, and the White Azalea plantation should be maintained and replaced when they show deterioration. The roses in the large central level of the terraces will inevitably become less important as the clipped box edging and free standing plants encroach on the smaller growth; but the proportion of the design should be kept and the edgings restrained from becoming hedges and the clipped plants from growing into trees, which would be too large in scale for the area.

Next came the keystone of her campus planting, provision for replacement.

In order to provide for replacement of the plants which seem inevitably associated with Dumbarton Oaks it may be wise to start a small nursery for Box, Yew, Holly, Oaks, and other plants which are costly to buy in large size.

And with the nursery proposal she suggested setting up a system for following the success or failure of specific plants—in other words, for the systematization of knowledge about the plants in place.

The start of a plant record book such as is found useful at the Universities of Chicago, Princeton and Yale is suggested. Such a book keeps in an easily accessible and yet alterable form a record of the different units, whether these be buildings and their surroundings, or open spaces, and the types of planting that have seemed fitting and effective.[74]

Nothing completes the picture of Farrand's approach to landscaping so well as her proposals for the transformation of Dumbarton Oaks. Here her university experience came to work to transform the private garden with which she had culminated her landscaping career into a public landscape (figs. 95 & 96). It is interesting to note that Reef Point Gardens, her own family garden in Maine, would follow a similar route. Hoping to preserve it by transferring it from private to public use, she tried to make it into an

95. The upper level of the North Vista at Dumbarton Oaks as modified in the transition to Harvard University. Plants have been added for screening. *Cedrus deodora* planted by Farrand is in the foreground. Photograph: Alan Ward.

educational institution, a botanical garden of Maine's native plants. Unfortunately, her personal resources were not sufficient to endow it adequately and it did not survive her. But Dumbarton Oaks, like her campuses, remains as evidence of her progress from landscape gardener to landscape architect of public institutions.

The Pierpont Morgan Library (1913–1943)

Between 1913 and 1943, Farrand designed and cared for the Pierpont Morgan Library garden (fig. 16). The job came to her because of the friendship and connections between her mother's family—the Cadwaladers—and J.

96. The lower level of the North Vista at Dumbarton Oaks subsequent to the transfer of the garden to Harvard University. Photograph: Alan Ward.

Pierpont Morgan, Sr. In a 1935 letter to Morgan's son, Beatrix Farrand mentioned "the many ties of affection between your family and mine,"[75] and in another noted that "Mr. Cadwalader [her uncle] and Mr. Morgan have shot at Millden Lodge in times past. Millden is next door to Mr. Morgan's shoot, Gannochy".[76]

This project is particularly interesting because it clearly illustrates what happened to landscape between the First World War and the end of the Second. With the coming of the Depression in 1930 and with the labor shortages later occasioned by war, landscape architecture changed dramatically. Landscapes designed for public use were the ones most affected by the changes. And the Morgan garden had essentially passed from private to public use when the Morgan Library, attached to the Morgan town house, was opened to the public in 1924.

J. Pierpont Morgan, Sr. commissioned Farrand to landscape his town house in 1913 and died in 1914. J. Pierpont Morgan, Jr. continued to support the upkeep of the garden but his interest in it diminished as time progressed.

In February of 1922, Farrand wrote to John Holmes, the business secretary of the estate. She mentioned the cost of replacing plants and trees in the garden. Many had been damaged "since growing conditions in the dust and laden smoke of New York City are most unfavorable to plant growth." Farrand justified the costs as usual: "Chrysanthemum planting of last Autumn was made after consultation with Mrs. Morgan and because she kindly wishes the garden to be as much pleasure to the passers-by in the streets as is reasonably possible."[77]

In 1934, Morgan's secretary brought up the issue of money in relation to labor. It became a more important issue with each passing year. By 1940, Mr. Morgan insisted, "some reduction ought to be made."[78] His proposal included firing the gardener and hiring a landscape company. Farrand interceded for the gardener. She proposed asking him to take a wage-cut rather than lose his job. She actually asked him to accept a decrease from $1,898 to $1,560 a year. This would be a saving over hiring the proposed landscape company, which charged $50.00 a month plus labor. In October, she told the secretary that the gardener had accepted "in the very best spirit possible," but this victory was short-lived. In September of 1941, the gardener was dismissed and the Roman Landscape Contracting Company started work. Farrand told Morgan's secretary that the landscaping company would come twice a week during the whole year except for summer, when it would come three days a week. "I hope Mr. Morgan is satisfied with the arrangement made which while not much of a saving at least will probably mean a few dollars less annual total."[79]

The Pierpont Morgan story may seem to be about people who were too much interested in cost-cutting and too little interested in landscaping. Yet this case is not unique. In every public project previously discussed we find similar things occurring: people had begun to question the labor costs

97. Drawing for the entrance to the Yale botanical garden. Courtesy of University of California, Berkeley; Department of Landscape Architecture; Documents Collection.

connected with public landscaping. Their answer was to organize work on different lines, replacing the landscapers and full-time gardeners who were trained to design and develop landscape with maintenance companies and machines. Yale, as previously noted, reduced its landscape staff from sixty to forty during the 1930s. Princeton had no purchase budget at all between 1922 and 1933, the campus nursery being the sole source of plants. At many colleges and universities, gardeners were replaced simply by maintenance people.

On 21 July 1943, Holmes wrote to Morgan and described complaints made by Library personnel. They clearly reveal that people were thinking differently about the way public landscape should be done.

Dear Commander Morgan:

I enclose a letter from Mrs. Farrand about the Garden. Not having any idea myself as to how many ivies would be the right number to make the place look right, I spoke to Miss Greene [director of the Library] about it. She was not able to be very helpful on that particular question, but she did say that both she and Mrs. Nichols have for some time been very

LE BOTANICAL GARDENS

> *critical of the condition in which the garden is kept, as compared with what it used to be. A large part of the answer no doubt lies in the fact that so much less is spent on the maintenance now; but Miss Greene thinks, as I do, that part of the difficulty is due to the fact that there is no one on the spot who has anything to do with the arrangements, or any authority over the people who have the work to do. Mrs. Farrand, of course, is able to make only very occasional visits there, and in between those visits there is no supervision. I am wondering whether it would not be better now to take the matter out of Mrs. Farrand's hands and make our own arrangements direct—either with the same people or with some other gardening company.*[80]

The Morgan Library story shows how the labor reorganization set in motion by the Industrial Revolution eventually affected landscaping. The "modern" method involved companies which owned heavy machinery that worked faster than human beings and decreased the need for human labor. An individual without specialized training or knowledge could execute maintenance work. This reorganization also replaced the landscaper: visits on a weekly basis by workmen from a landscaping company would be more productive than three or four yearly visits by a professional. The professional's work could be reduced to the initial planting and perhaps a yearly visit.

Universities with large campuses followed a similar course: they purchased mechanical equipment and set up maintenance schedules. The landscape professional had much less say, and more to the point, could not carry out a program of planting and designing that spanned many years. The landscape designer was now involved only with the initial planting. Maintenance and replacement work was left to others. Money was saved, but in the process, a sense of direction was lost. As control was dissipated, public landscapes no longer reflected a clear aim or purpose.

Clearly, the changes brought about by the Depression make it impossible to return to the old ways of doing landscape work. But our current solution for public landscape also has failed. A method should be devised for continuity of design and maintenance that spans the life of a public landscape.

Farrand's principles and sound horticultural methods give us a clear outline of what is needed. In her passage from private residential gardens to public landscapes we find a clear statement of aim, philosophy, and method. The method is still valid; so is the ideal. Through the example of Farrand's campus work, we may find the perfect instrument to preserve and create America's public landscapes.

APPENDIX

BEATRIX FARRAND'S COMMISSIONS 1891–1949

Following is a list, compiled chronologically, of Beatrix Farrand's work in landscape and garden design, beginning in 1891 when she was nineteen years old and ending in 1949 when she was seventy-seven. Commissions for which the dates are unknown will be found at the end of the list. Indication of continuing work is given in parentheses following the name of the commission.

1891

Crosswicks; Residence of Clement B. Newbold, Jenkintown, Pennsylvania (1891–1916)

1896

Residence of William R. Garrison, Tuxedo Park, New York (1896–1899)

Tuxedo Village (location unknown)

1897

Lych Gate, Seal Harbor, Maine

Residence of Trenor L. Park, Harrison, New York (1897–1898)

1898

Residence of Dr. E. K. Dunham, Seal Harbor, Maine

Greenfield Hill Schoolhouse, Greenfield Hill, Connecticut

Residence of Mrs. Elizabeth Hope Slater, Newport, Rhode Island

1899

Residence of Dr. C. Dunham, Irvington-on-Hudson, New York (1899–1900)

Belle-Haven; Residence of Nathaniel Witherell, Greenwich, Connecticut (1899–1900)

1900

Residence of E. C. Bodman, Seal Harbor, Maine

Residence of Percy Chubb, Dosoris, Long Island, New York

Residence of H. R. Hatfield, Bar Harbor, Maine

1901

Residence of Robert Abbe, Bar Harbor, Maine

Residence of Gordon Bell, Ridgefield, Connecticut

Chiltern; Residence of Edgar T. Scott, Bar Harbor, Maine (1901–1912)

Residence of Edward Wharton, Lenox, Massachusetts

1902

Residence of George S. Bowdoin, Bar Harbor, Maine

Protestant Episcopal Cathedral, Washington, District of Columbia

Residence of Arson Phelps Stokes, Darien, Connecticut

1903

Residence of E. G. Fabbri, Bar Harbor, Maine

1905

Residence of Mrs. Ines Roswell Eldridge, Great Neck, New York (1905–1930)

The Roland Park Women's Club (location unknown)

1906

Residence of William F. Apthorp, Hulls Cove, Maine

Residence of John D. Rockefeller, Jr., Pocantico Hills, New York

Residence of Edward F. Whitney, Oyster Bay, New York (1906–1914)

1908

Residence of Mrs. A. T. Mahan, Quogue, Long Island, New York

Woodburne; Residence of Edgar Scott, Lansdowne, Pennsylvania (1908–1909)

Residence of William Douglas Sloane, Lenox, Massachusetts

1909

Harston; Residence of Henry F. Harris, Chestnut Hill, Pennsylvania (1909–1911)

Office and/or Residence of Dr. Frederick Peterson and Dr. James Markoe, 20 West 50th Street, New York, New York

Hillcrest; Residence of William A. Read, Harrison, New York (1909–1927)

1910

Residence of William Bayard Cutting, Oakdale, Long Island, New York

Residence of Harris Fahnestock, Lenox, Massachusetts (1910–1914)

Residence of Mrs. Henry Cabot Lodge, Nahant, Massachusetts (1910–1911)

1911

Residence of Mrs. Philip W. Livermore, Jericho, Long Island, New York

Residence of John K. Mitchell, III, Villanova, Pennsylvania (1911–1912)

1912

Residence of Sherman Flint, Islip, Long Island, New York

Residence of Robert Goelet, Glenmere, New York (1912–1916)

Miss Hillard's School for Girls, Middlebury, Connecticut

Residence of Robert L. Montgomery, Villanova, Pennsylvania

Residence of Thomas Newbold, Hyde Park, New York

Princeton University, Princeton, New Jersey (1912–1943)
St. Paul's Church, Red Hook, New York
Residence of Clarence A. Warden, Haverford, Pennsylvania (1912–1932)

1913

Residence of J. Pierpont Morgan (later the Pierpont Morgan Library), New York, New York (1913–1943)
Tennis Shelter for Mrs. J. Montgomery Sears, Southboro, Massachusetts
The White House; for Mrs. Woodrow Wilson, Washington, District of Columbia (1913–1916)

1914

Reef Point; Residence of Beatrix Farrand, Bar Harbor, Maine (1914–1928)
Residence of C. Oliver Iselin, Brookville, Long Island, New York
Residence of Mrs. George D. Pratt, Glen Cove, Long Island, New York
Residence of M. Taylor Pyne, Princeton, New Jersey
Straight Improvement Co. Inc. (Willard D. Straight) and/or Dorothy Whitney (Straight) Elmhirst, Old Westbury, Long Island, New York (1914–1932)

1915

Residence of Thomas Hastings, Roslyn, Long Island, New York
New Haven Hospital Tuberculosis Annex, West Haven, Connecticut (1915–1916)
Rose Garden; New York Botanical Garden, Bronx, New York (1915–1916)
Residence of Professor F. W. Williams, Whitney Avenue, New Haven, Connecticut (1915–1916)

1916

Residence of John F. Braun, Merion, Pennsylvania (1916–1917)

1917

Rockefeller Institute for Medical Research (RIMR), Plainsboro, New Jersey (1917–1921)
Residence of Frank Bailey Rowell, Bar Harbor, Maine
Tanglewold; Residence of Mrs. A. Murray Young, Bar Harbor, Maine

1918

Grove Point; Residence of S. Vernon Mann, Great Neck, New York (1918–1930)

1919

Residence of Mrs. Samuel G. Colt, Pittsfield, Massachusetts (1919–1924)
Residence of Mrs. Zenas Crane, Dalton, Massachusetts (1919–1924)
The Ethel Walker School, Simsbury, Connecticut
Eolia; Residence of Edward S. Harkness, New London, Connecticut (1919–1932)
Residence of Otto Kahn, Cold Spring Harbor, New York (1919–1928)
Residence of Mrs. Dave Hennen Morris, Bar Harbor, Maine
Residence of Mrs. F. B. Richard, Blue Hill, Maine

1920

Residence of Mrs. Hanna, Seal Harbor, Maine
Montevideo; Residence of O. F. Roberts, Simsbury, Connecticut

1921

The Oaks (now Dumbarton Oaks); Residence of Robert Woods Bliss, Washington, District of Columbia (1921–1947)
Residence of William Adams Delano, Syosset, Long Island, New York
The Old Adam House; Residence of Mrs. Richard Derby, Oyster Bay, New York
Residence of Edward S. Harkness, Manhasset, Long Island, New York
Easthold; Residence of Richard M. Hoe, Seal Harbor, Maine (1921–1924)
Three Rivers Farm; Residence of Dr. Frederick Peterson, Shepaug, Connecticut (1921–1922)
Residence of Mrs. Herbert L. Satterlee, Bar Harbor, Maine (1921–1939)

1922

Village Green and Athletic Field, Bar Harbor, Maine
Residence of Mrs. Samuel H. Fisher, Litchfield, Connecticut (1922–1929)
Great Neck Green, Great Neck, Long Island, New York(1922–1932)
The Hill School, Pottstown, Pennsylvania (1922–1935)
Residence of Mrs. A. G. Thacher, Bar Harbor, Maine
Yale University, New Haven, Connecticut (1922–1945)

1923

Residence of Miss Anne Baker (location unknown)
Residence of Parker Corning, Bar Harbor, Maine (1923–1925)
Residence of Mrs. Mildred McCormick, Bar Harbor, Maine (1923–1928)
Residence of Gerrish H. Milliken, 723 Park Avenue, New York, New York (1923–1930)
The Phelps Association, New Haven, Connecticut (1923–1933)
Residence of Rush Sturges, Power Street, Providence, Rhode Island
Residence of Nelson B. Williams, Bedford, New York

1924

Residence of Walter Ayer, Bar Harbor, Maine (1924–1925)
Winter Palace; Residence of Cortlandt F. Bishop, Lenox, Massachusetts (1924–1925)
Hamilton College, Clinton, New York
Seal Harbor Green, Seal Harbor, Maine

1925

Residence of Mrs. William H. Bliss, Montecito, California
Great Neck Green Public Library, Great Neck, Long Island, New York (1925–1932)
Merion Cricket Club Golf Association, Haverford, Pennsylvania
The Haven; Residence of Gerrish H. Milliken, Northeast Harbor, Maine (1925–1945)
Residence of D. H. Morris, Glen Head, Long Island, New York
Residence of Percy R. Pyne, Roslyn, Long Island, New York (1925–1929)

1926

Residence of Mrs. William G. Beale (location unknown)
Residence of Mr. Jacob S. Disston, Northeast Harbor, Maine
Residence of Mrs. Bradford Fraley, Northeast Harbor, Maine
Residence of Mr. Robert McCormick, Bar Harbor, Maine (1926–1936)

The Eyrie Garden; Residence of John D. Rockefeller, Jr., Seal Harbor, Maine (1926–1950)

Vassar College, Poughkeepsie, New York (1926–1927)

Residence of Mrs. Charlton Yarnall, Northeast Harbor, Maine (1926–1927)

1927

Residence of Edward J. Hancy (location unknown)

Residence of William Pierson Hamilton, Bar Harbor, Maine (1927–1928)

Residence of Mrs. Morris Hawkes, Bar Harbor, Maine (1927–1928)

Residence of H. E. Manville, Pleasantville, New York (1927–1928)

Residence of Vance McCormick, Northeast Harbor, Maine (1927–1935)

Rockhurst; Residence of Charles E. Sampson, Bar Harbor, Maine (1927–1936)

Residence of Charles Wheeler, Bryn Mawr, Pennsylvania (1927–1928)

1928

Residence of Mrs. Byrne, Bar Harbor, Maine

California Institute of Technology, Pasadena, California (1928–1938)

Solar Laboratory for Dr. G. E. Hale, Pasadena, California

Residence of Potter Palmer, Bar Harbor, Maine (1928–1929)

Residence of E. T. Stotesbury, Bar Harbor, Maine (1928–1931)

Oakpoint; Residence of Harrison Williams, Bayville, Long Island, New York (1928–1929)

1929

Residence of Mrs. Gano Dunn, Sutton's Island, Maine

Cemetery plot for Edward S. Harkness, Woodlawn Cemetery, New York (1929–1933)

Kings Point; Residence of S. Vernon Mann, Jr., Nassau County, New York

Residence of Henry Rawle, Northeast Harbor, Maine (1929–1930)

Residence of Robert I. Rogers, Beverly Hills, California

The University of Chicago, Chicago, Illinois (1929–1936)

1930

Residence of W. Barton Eddison, Northeast Harbor, Maine

Henry E. Huntington Library and Art Gallery, San Marino, California (1930–1935)

Holm Lea; Residence of Miss Alice Sargent, Brookline, Massachusetts

1931

Arnold House; Residence of Harry G. Haskell, Northeast Harbor, Maine

Pennsylvania School of Horticulture for Women, Ambler, Pennsylvania (1931–1932)

1932

Northeast Harbor Tennis Club, Northeast Harbor, Maine (1932–1934)

Ste. Marguerite Salmon Club, Riviere Ste. Marguerite, Tadousac, Quebec, Canada

Henry Whitfield State Historical Museum, Guilford, Connecticut

1933

Dartington Hall, Ltd., Totnes, Devonshire, England (1933–1938)

1934

Churston Development Co., Ltd., Dartington Hall, Totnes, Devonshire, England

1936

Casa Dorinda; Residence of Mrs. William H. Bliss, Santa Barbara, California

Residence of Rush Sturges, South Kensington, Rhode Island

1937

Edgewood Park; New Haven Parks Department, New Haven, Connecticut

Residence of Gerrish H. Milliken, Greenwich, Connecticut

Occidental College, Los Angeles, California (1937–1940)

1938

Palomar Mountain Observatory Site, California Institute of Technology

1939

Oberlin College, Oberlin, Ohio (1939–1946)

1942

Residence of Michael Straight, Fairfax County, Virginia

1949

Guest House of David Rockefeller, Seal Harbor, Maine

UNDATED COMMISSIONS

Augusta Maine, State Park

Residence of Dr. J. C. Ayer, Glen Cove, Long Island, New York

Residence of Robert P. Bowler, Bar Harbor, Maine

Residence of Eugene S. Bristol, Bar Harbor, Maine

Residence of A. M. Coats (location unknown)

Stoney Point; Residence of Mrs. Edwin Corning, Northeast Harbor, Maine

Residence of Albert Craisse (location unknown)

Residence of T. W. Farnam, 328 Temple Street, New Haven, Connecticut

Residence of Giraud Foster, Lenox, Massachusetts

Residence of William Pierson Hamilton, Sterlington, New York

Residence of C. A. Herter, Seal Harbor, Maine

Residence of J. Ramsay Hunt (location unknown)

Residence of Emma J. Martin, Spring Lake, New Jersey

Residence of Mrs. Gerrish H. Milliken, Sterling Falls, Armonk, New York

Woodlands; Residence of William S. Moore, Bar Harbor, Maine

Mount Desert Island Hospital, Bar Harbor, Maine

Residence of Mrs. Douglas W. Paige, Bellport, Long Island, New York

Residence of Mrs. Phillips, North Beverly, Massachusetts

Residence of Henry Rawle, Morristown, New Jersey

Residence of Geraldyn Redmond, Tivoli, New York

Residence of Mrs. J. W. Riddle, Farmington, Connecticut

Residence of C. C. Stillman, Cornwall, New York

Residence of Mrs. J. C. Thaw, Southampton, Long Island, New York

Residence of J. J. Van Alen, Newport, Rhode Island

NOTES

The following abbreviations have been used in the citations below:

BFF/PMLA	Beatrix Farrand file, Pierpont Morgan Library Archive
BFF/PUA	Beatrix Farrand file, Princeton University Archive
CIT	California Institute of Technology
CUA	University of Chicago Archive
OCA	Oberlin College Archive
RMP/CIT	Robert Millikan Papers, California Institute of Technology
SBBG	Santa Barbara Botanic Garden
TR/YU	Treasurer's Records, Yale University
UCal	Documents Collection, Department of Landscape Architecture, University of California, Berkeley
YU	Yale University

A Biographical Note and a Consideration of Four Major Private Gardens

ELEANOR M. MCPECK

1. The biographical portion of this chapter is a revision and expansion of two earlier articles by the author: "Beatrix Jones Farrand" in *Notable American Women* (Cambridge, Mass., Belknap Press of Harvard University Press, 1980) and "Beatrix Jones Farrand; the Formative Years" in *Beatrix Jones Farrand: Fifty Years of American Landscape Architecture* (Washington, D.C., Dumbarton Oaks, 1982). I wish to thank Dumbarton Oaks, Trustees for Harvard University and the Harvard University Press for permission to incorporate here much of the material previously published. I also wish to thank the following individuals for their assistance in my research: David Wright, Archivist, Pierpont Morgan Library; Elisabeth MacDougall, Director of

Studies in Landscape Architecture, Laura Byers, Garden Librarian, and Judith Bloomgarden, Dumbarton Oaks; Thomas Rosenbaum, Archivist, Rockefeller Archive Center; William Howard Adams; Peter Johnson; Elizabeth Baumgartner; Susan Vutz and Annemarie Adams, Documents Collection, Department of Landscape Architecture, University of California, Berkeley; Gould Colman, Department of Manuscripts and University Archives, Cornell University; Michael Straight; Robert W. Patterson; and Paula Dietz.

2. R. W. B. Lewis, *Edith Wharton; a Biography* (New York, 1975): 26.

3. "In Memory of Mary Cadwalader Jones, December Twelfth 1850–September Twenty Second 1935." Remembrances by friends delivered at a memorial service at the Church of the Ascension, New York City, 12 December 1935. Typescript. UCal.

4. Henry W. Taft. "John Lambert Cadwalader; an Appreciation." Read at the opening of the Trenton Public Library, 6 April 1915. New York Public Library.

5. Mildred B. Bliss, "An Attempted Evocation of a Personality," *Landscape Architecture* (Summer 1959): 218.

6. Leon Edel, *Henry James, the Master; 1901–1916* (New York, 1972): 200.

7. Ibid.

8. Ibid.: 203.

9. Ibid.: 287.

10. Henry James, *Letters,* ed. Leon Edel (Cambridge, Mass., 1984): 4:338.

11. Mrs. Winthrop Chanler, *Roman Spring* (Boston, 1934):269.

12. BFF/PMLA.

13. Robert W. Patterson, "Beatrix Farrand 1872–1959; an Appreciation of a Great Landscape Gardener," *Landscape Architecture* (Summer 1959): 217.

14. Ibid.: 216.

15. Beatrix Farrand, "Beatrix Farrand, 1872–1959," *Reef Point Gardens Bulletin* 1, no. 17 (n.d.). This is a posthumously published autobiographical note, written in the third person.

16. Ibid.

17. Beatrix Jones [Farrand], Journal, 2 June 1893. UCal.

18. Ibid., 9 June 1892.

19. Ibid., 30 March 1895.

20. Ibid., 27 March 1895.

21. Ibid., 2 April 1895.

22. Ibid., 12 May 1895.

23. Gertrude Jekyll, *On Gardening*, ed. Elizabeth Lawrence (New York, 1964): 23–24.

24. Beatrix Jones [Farrand] in *Garden and Forest* (15 January 1896): 22.

25. Beatrix Jones [Farrand], interview in the *New York Herald Tribune,* 11 February 1900.

26. Edith Wharton and Ogden Codman, *The Decoration of Houses* (New York, 1897): 2.

27. Ibid., 198.

28. Edith Wharton, *Italian Villas and Their Gardens* (New York, 1905): 8.

29. Beatrix Jones [Farrand], "The Garden in Relation to the House," *Garden and Forest* (7 April 1897): 132–33.

30. Beatrix Jones [Farrand], "The Garden as a Picture," *Scribner's* (1906): 5.

31. Patterson, "Appreciation," 218.

32. Dictionary of American Biography.

33. Patterson, "Appreciation," 218.

34. Michael Straight, letter to the author, 16 January 1980.

35. Beatrix Jones [Farrand], "Laying Out a Suburban Place," *Country Life* (March 1910): 551.

36. Ibid.

37. Ibid.: 552.

38. BFF/PMLA. All correspondence

between Farrand and the Morgan family or staff that I have quoted will be found in this file.

39. Straight Improvement Co., file 1003, UCal.

40. Anne Baker to Beatrix Farrand, undated, but probably 1924. UCal.

41. Anne Baker to Beatrix Farrand, 17 November 1924. UCal.

42. O. Gorton (Dorothy Straight's secretary) to Anne Baker, 19 February 1925. UCal.

43. Michael Straight, letter to the author, 16 January 1980.

44. Rockefeller Family Archive. Record Group 2. Office of the Messrs. Rockefeller. Homes Series, Subseries Seal Harbor Maine. Rockefeller Archive Center. All correspondence concerning the Rockefeller estate at Seal Harbor quoted here will be found in this record group.

45. Bliss, "Attempted Evocation," 223.

46. Georgina Masson, *Dumbarton Oaks; a Guide to the Gardens* (Washington, D.C., 1968).

47. Patterson, "Appreciation," 218.

48. Masson, *Dumbarton Oaks,* 21.

49. *Beatrix Farrand's Plant Book for Dumbarton Oaks* (Washington D.C., 1980): 127–29.

Plants and Planting Design

DIANE KOSTIAL MCGUIRE

1. Gertrude Jekyll, *Colour Schemes for the Flower Garden,* 8th ed. (London, 1936): 3.

2. Gertrude Jekyll, *Wood and Garden* (London, 1899): 264.

3. *Beatrix Farrand's Plant Book for Dumbarton Oaks* (Washington, D.C., 1980): 63–64.

4. Thomas Mawson, *The Art and Craft of Garden Making* (London, 1900): x.

5. Ibid.: ix.

6. Jekyll, *Wood and Garden*, 266.

7. Herman Muthesius, *The English House* (New York, 1979):9.

8. Farrand, *Plant Book*, 69.

9. Ibid.: 67–69.

10. Jekyll, *Wood and Garden,* 157.

11. Beatrix Farrand to Anne Sweeney, 11 October 1941. Dumbarton Oaks Garden Library.

12. Isabel Zucker, *Flowering Shrubs* (Princeton, 1966): 218.

13. Farrand, *Plant Book,* 32.

14. Helen van Pelt Wilson, *The Fragrant Year* (New York, 1967): 33.

15. Farrand, *Plant Book,* 37.

Campus Work and Public Landscapes

DIANA BALMORI

1. I would like to thank the following individuals for their help at various stages of my research: Jedda Ziolkowski at Princeton University; John Wisnewski, George Clarke, and John Melody, of the staff at Princeton, who supplied details on landscaping operations at the university, past and present; Earle Coleman, Princeton's Archivist; James Clark, former Head Gardener at Princeton and Thomas Kane, the landscape architect who led me to him; Patricia Stark and Tawney Nelb of the Sterling Memorial Library at Yale University; Christopher Yulo and Jonathan Cummings, Yale students who served as research assistants; Jean Block and Daniel Meyer, archivists at the University of Chicago; Jane Goodstein

and Carol Buge of the California Institute of Technology; Christine Flack Vail Shirley, the recent purchaser of the George E. Hale Solar Observatory; Katherine Muller of the Santa Barbara Botanic Garden; Frances Mason and David Wright at the Pierpont Morgan Library; Elisabeth MacDougall, Director of Studies in Landscape Architecture, and Laura Byers, Garden Librarian, at Dumbarton Oaks; photographer Alan Ward; and for permission to photograph at Princeton, George Eager, and at Yale, Jack Kirby; Michael Laurie of the School of Environmental Design, University of California, Berkeley, and Susan Vutz and Stephen Tobriner at the Documents Collection there.

2. The epithet was brought to my attention by professors Willard Thorpe at Princeton and George Pierson at Yale. They knew Farrand when she worked at their respective campuses and heard her called by this name.

3. Alexander Leitch, *A Princeton Companion* (Princeton, 1978): 74–79.

4. Beatrix Farrand, Report to Oberlin College, 23 June 1939. OCA.

5. Beatrix Farrand to Mrs. Luther Pfahler Eisenhart, Wyman House, 11 December 1934. BFF/PUA.

6. W. H. Laverty, University of Chicago Department of Buildings and Grounds. Notes on Mrs. Farrand's Visit, 20 April 1936. Vertical File, UCal.

7. Beatrix Farrand to Thomas Farnam, Comptroller, 31 December 1925. TR/YU.

8. Beatrix Farrand to Lester Ries, Department of Buildings and Grounds, 21 August 1942. File 715, Box 150, OCA.

9. Beatrix Farrand to Donald M. Love, 21 August 1942. OCA.

10. Farrand, Oberlin Report: 2.

11. Beatrix Farrand to Thomas Farnam, 4 December 1923. TR/YU.

12. Princeton University Notes, 3 November 1936: 6. BFF/PUA.

13. Princeton University Notes, 13 November 1935: 6. BFF/PUA.

14. Beatrix Farrand to Thomas Farnam, 17 March 1923. TR/YU.

15. William B. Munro to Beatrix Farrand, 19 November 1938. Box 18, RMP/CIT.

16. Points agreed upon at Conference held 20 January 1948. SBBG.

17. Princeton University Notes, 3 November 1936: 3. BFF/PUA.

18. Princeton University Notes, 22–26 October 1937: 2. BFF/PUA.

19. Princeton University Notes, 24 October 1938: 4. BFF/PUA.

20. Princeton University Notes, 4 July 1933:11. BFF/PUA.

21. *Yale Alumni Weekly* (15 April 1927): 816.

22. Beatrix Farrand to Thomas Farnam, 21 November 1922. TR/YU.

23. Princeton University Notes, 3 November 1936:7. BFF/PUA.

24. Princeton University Notes, 19 November 1934:5. BFF/PUA.

25. Beatrix Farrand to E. A. MacMillan, 31 January 1933. BFF/PUA.

26. Beatrix Farrand to Yale University, 5 July 1922. TR/YU.

27. *Yale Alumni Weekly* (15 April 1927): 815.

28. Princeton University Notes, 30 May 1936: 2. BFF/PUA.

29. Beatrix Farrand to Thomas Farnam, 8 April 1924. TR/YU.

30. W. H. Laverty, University of Chicago Department of Buildings and Grounds. Notes on Mrs. Farrand's Visit, 20 April 1936. Vertical File, UCal.

31. University of Chicago Trustees Minutes. Committee of Buildings and Grounds. 20 March 1930:6. CUA.

32. Jean Block, University of Chicago Archivist, to the author, 12 September 1984.

33. Beatrix Farrand to Thomas Farnam, 18 October 1922. TR/YU.

34. Oberlin College to Beatrix Farrand, 21 January 1941. File 7–1–15, Box 150, OCA.

35. Ruth Havey, interview with the author at Dumbarton Oaks, May 1980.

36. Beatrix Farrand to Robert A. Millikan, 24 March 1938. Box 18, RMP/CIT.

37. Ibid.

38. Beatrix Farrand to William B. Munro, 19 July 1938. Box 18, RMP/CIT.

39. Beatrix Farrand to Dorothy Skinner, 28 July 1933. Box 5, Folder 6, Buildings and Grounds Department Records, CU.

40. Diana Balmori, "Beatrix Farrand at Dumbarton Oaks: The Design Process of a Garden," in *Beatrix Jones Farrand: Fifty Years of American Landscape Architecture* (Washington, D.C., 1982): 120–21.

41. Beatrix Jones [Farrand] to G. C. Wintringer, 27 June 1912. BFF/PUA.

42. Professor Willard Thorpe, interview with the author, 11 October 1984.

43. Beatrix Jones [Farrand], Report to Princeton University, 28 October 1912. BFF/PUA.

44. Beatrix Farrand, Report Submitted to the Grounds and Building Committee, Princeton University, 27 December 1913. BFF/PUA.

45. Ralph Adams Cram to Henry B. Thompson, member of the Princeton Buildings and Grounds Committee, 27 December 1912. BFF/PUA.

46. Unsigned letter to Charles Hart, Philadelphia. Comparison with other letters in the same format and using the same typewriter shows that it is a letter from E. A. MacMillan, Superintendent of Grounds and Buildings at Princeton. BFF/PUA.

47. Beatrix Farrand, "Landscape Gardening at Princeton," *Princeton Alumni Weekly* (29 May 1931).

48. Beatrix Farrand to Henry S. Graves, 15 April 1925. TR/YU.

49. Henry S. Graves to George Parmly Day on the Botanical Garden & Arboretum, 8 October 1923. TR/YU.

50. Beatrix Farrand to Thomas Farnam, 24 July 1923. TR/YU.

51. School of Forestry to Charles Sargent, 12 January 1925. TR/YU.

52. F. B. Johnson, University Service Bureaus, to Thomas Farnam, 23 November 1922. TR/YU.

53. Beatrix Farrand to Henry S. Graves, 15 April 1925. TR/YU.

54. Beatrix Farrand to Dean C. Winternitz, 26 May 1924. TR/YU.

55. Thomas Farnam to Beatrix Farrand, 8 January 1925. TR/YU.

56. George A. Cromie to President James R. Angell, 1 November 1934. Angell Presidential Papers, YU.

57. George Cromie, Weekly Landscape Report, 7 March 1932. Angell Presidential Papers, YU.

58. Jean F. Block, *The Uses of Gothic; Planning and Building the Campus of the University of Chicago, 1892–1932* (Chicago: University of Chicago Library, 1983): 7.

59. University of Chicago Trustees Minutes. Committee on Buildings and Grounds. 23 December 1929: 9 CUA.

60. W. H. Laverty, University of Chicago Department of Buildings and Grounds. Notes on Mrs. Farrand's Visit, 20 April 1936. Vertical File, UCal.

61. University of Chicago Notes on Mrs. Farrand's Visit, 27–28 March 1936. UCal.

62. Donald Love, Secretary, Oberlin College, to Beatrix Farrand, 21 February 1939. File 7–1–5, Box 150, OCA.

63. Beatrix Farrand to Donald Love, 20 May 1939. File 7–1–5, Box 150, OCA.

64. The buildings listed by Farrand are: three new fraternity and eight faculty houses; area between Library and Hall of Science; between Library and Knox; south side of Hockey Rink; between Knox and Commons; Chapel; North; Hall of Philosophy; South College; Carnegie; Hall of Science; Commons; Y.M.C.A.; Biology-Geology; Library; Chemistry; Rocky Building-Sage. The planting list is undated but the survey plan for Hamilton is dated 1924. Vertical file, UCal.

65. Walter Pilkington, *Hamilton College: a History* (Clinton, 1962): 235.

66. Mrs. Farrand's Suggestions for Improving the Western Portion of the Campus. Report accompanying letter from W. B. Munro to R. A. Millikan, 1 February 1935. Box 18, RMP/CIT.

67. Beatrix Farrand to R. A. Millikan, 15 June 1934. Box 18, RMP/CIT.

68. California Institute of Technology Trustees Minutes, 6 July 1937: 11. CIT.

69. Professor Glenn Geer, Department of Horticulture, Temple University, to the author. Professor Geer also furnished the photographs.

70. Marlene Salon, "Beatrix Farrand, Landscape Gardener." Master's Thesis, Syracuse University. Also her "Beatrix Farrand: Pioneer in Gilt-Edged Gardens," *Landscape Architecture* (January 1977): 69–77.

71. Richard A. Lyon, "The Campus Designs of Beatrix Farrand," in *Beatrix Jones Farrand: Fifty Years of American Landscape Architecture* (Washington, D.C., 1982): 55.

72. Paul Venable Turner, *Campus: an American Planning Tradition* (Cambridge, Mass., 1984): 106.

73. All material cited is from three reports made by Farrand and De Forest dated 12 March 1939, 20 December 1943, and 28 February 1944. SBBG.

74. *Beatrix Farrand's Plant Book for Dumbarton Oaks* (Washington, D.C., 1980).

75. Beatrix Farrand to J. P. Morgan, Jr., 15 December 1935. BFF/PMLA.

76. Beatrix Farrand to J. Axten, secretary to Morgan, 17 September 1935. BFF/PMLA.

77. Beatrix Farrand to John Holmes, 6 February 1922. BFF/PMLA.

78. John Holmes to Beatrix Farrand, 25 September 1940. BFF/PMLA.

79. All correspondence relating to this matter can be found in BFF/PMLA.

80. John Holmes to J. P. Morgan, 21 July 1943. BFF/PMLA.

INDEX

NOTES ON THE AUTHORS

DIANA BALMORI is a partner in the firm of Cesar Pelli and Associates where she has joined in designing the Museum of Modern Art expansion. She is partner-in-charge for landscape design. She has also lectured frequently on the history of landscape architecture at Yale University, New York University, and SUNY-Oswego, and she was a contributor to the publication *Beatrix Jones Farrand; Fifty Years of American Landscape Architecture* (Dumbarton Oaks, 1982).

DIANE KOSTIAL MCGUIRE is a principal, with Barbara Harrison Watson, in her own landscape-architecture firm. She serves as Professor of Landscape Architecture at the University of Arkansas and as Garden Advisor at Dumbarton Oaks. She was the editor of *Beatrix Farrand's Plant Book for Dumbarton Oaks* (Dumbarton Oaks, 1980) and was co-editor of *Beatrix Jones Farrand; Fifty Years of American Landscape Architecture*, to which she also contributed an essay.

ELEANOR M. MCPECK is a landscape designer, Instructor in Landscape History at the Radcliffe Seminars at Radcliffe College, and a former Dumbarton Oaks Garden Fellow. She wrote the biography of Beatrix Farrand in *Notable American Women* (Harvard University Press, 1980) and she, too, was author of a paper published in *Beatrix Jones Farrand; Fifty Years of American Landscape Architecture.*